CHESS FOR BEGINNERS

CHESS
FOR BEGINNERS

P. H. Clarke

COLLINS
LONDON & GLASGOW

Originally published in 1967 as a
Collins Nutshell book under the title *Chess*
This revised edition first published 1973

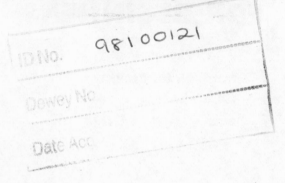

ISBN 0 00 410582 6

© Wm. Collins Sons & Co. Ltd. 1973

Printed in Great Britain by Collins Clear-Type Press

Contents

FOREWORD

Once a pastime at the courts of kings, chess is now a source of pleasure to countless people from every walk of life. As a game of skill it is unrivalled, possessing not only a depth that continually challenges the mind but also a logical simplicity and beauty. Elements of sport, science and even art are united in it.

The extraordinary complexity of chess cannot be denied, but that ought never to put off those who would like to try their hand at it. They will be able to enjoy the game at whatever level of play they reach, and learning the rules is by no means the painful process that many imagine it to be. On the contrary, the beginner need take but a few, easy steps to find himself on the threshold of a surprising and fascinating new world.

One of the most rewarding things about chess is that the better you play the greater the satisfaction it gives. For that reason it is worth cultivating a sound approach from the very start. The learner is advised to acquire the habit of going over his games afterwards and comparing them with examples from books, of which there is a particularly wide selection. It has been claimed, indeed, that more have been written about chess than there have about all other games added together—an exaggeration, no doubt, but not as absurd as it may at first appear.

The purpose of this book, which obviously can only scratch the surface of so vast a subject, is to provide a general introduction to chess and at the same time give the reader an insight into some of the game's finer points. While a considerable amount of factual knowledge or 'theory' has been included, special care has been taken to

7

explain the ideas and principles behind the moves; for they alone can impart a proper understanding. In this connection the chapter of classic games is important: through them and the accompanying notes, designed mainly to illustrate how the master tackles the problems facing him, a picture is built up of what is meant by good technique and style.

Those readers who are keen enough to want to increase their skill and knowledge by further study will find a list of recommended works at the end of the book. Chess offers an endless outlet for personal expression, both competitive and creative, and it is my hope that the following pages will stimulate you to discover some of its riches for yourself.

P.H.C.

1

INTRODUCING THE GAME

As near as the historian can determine, the game of chess originated in Northwest India at about the turn of the fifth century A.D. Story has it that its inventor wished to portray a battle between Indian forces of the time as a game; he called it *chaturanga*, a word which meant 'army' in Sanskrit.

Chaturanga, which differed remarkably little from modern chess, quickly spread out from India, westward into Persia, where it was known in the sixth century, and eastward into China and the rest of Asia. The conquest of Persia by Islam in the first half of the seventh century brought the game to the Arabs, and they took it into Europe via the Mediterranean. By 1100 A.D. it had reached the greater part of the civilised world, having come to England with the Normans. In this early period of its history the game was found in at least as many variants as countries where it was played, and such a state of affairs existed until roughly two hundred years ago. By that time the improvements and refinements evolved from advances in knowledge and skill had been accepted by most players and chess had assumed the form which is now internationally recognised.

The four basic elements of the Indian army and *chaturanga* were infantry, cavalry, chariots and elephants, and these are represented in chess by the pawns, Knights, Rooks and Bishops respectively. They were led by a King aided by a minister (the modern Queen). The field of combat became the chessboard, consisting of sixty-four

1. The Initial Postion

Each side has 1 King , 1 Queen , 2 Bishops , 2 Knights , 2 Rooks , and 8 pawns . Note that the Kings stand directly opposite one another and that each Queen starts on a square of its own colour.

squares (8 x 8) shaded alternately light and dark. The chessmen are also coloured in the same way, and from this we get the terms 'White' and 'Black' which refer to the two sides.

At the start of the game the board must be so placed between the players that each has a white square in the corner nearest his right hand. The opposing 'armies' are then drawn up as shown in Diagram 1. It is conventional for the white men to commence at the bottom of such diagrams and the black at the top; this will be observed throughout the present book.

Since the death or capture of the King was decisive in early Indian battles, it was natural that this means of victory should be applied in *chaturanga* and handed down to chess. The object of the game, therefore, is to bring about a situation where the enemy King can no longer avoid being captured. This is called 'checkmate' and will be explained in detail later in the chapter.

Play proceeds by 'moves' (the transfer of a man from one square to another) which may or may not involve the capture of opposing men. The players move alternately throughout the game, but White always goes first in the initial position. As the various men move in different

10

ways, it is necessary to examine each one and its powers separately.

The Rook

In the ancient game the Rook (the word is derived from the Persian for chariot—*rukh*) was the most powerful piece on the board. Though it now yields first place in that respect to the Queen, the straightforward character of its move makes the Rook the model of mobility in chess. It moves either vertically or horizontally for any number of squares in the same direction, as illustrated in Diagram 2. A unique feature of the Rook is that it commands the same number of squares (i.e. 14) wherever it stands.

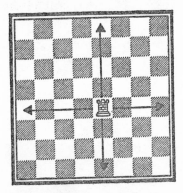

2. Rook Moves
The arrows indicate the extent of the Rook's moves. They also delineate a 'file' (a vertical row of squares) and a 'rank' (a horizontal row). The Rook can move vertically to anywhere else on the same file and horizontally along the same rank.

The Bishop

The Bishop's move is also rectilinear and as such complements that of the Rook. The Bishop moves diagonally for any number of squares in the same direction, as illustrated in Diagram 3. However, the Bishop is weaker than the Rook on two counts: first, its range depends on where it is situated (at the edge of the board it commands only 7 squares, whereas this figure rises to 13 when the Bishop stands in the centre); second, a Bishop that begins

11

the game on a white square can never transfer to a black square, and *vice versa* (consequently, its movements are limited to just half the board). The latter weakness is offset initially by the fact that each side's Bishops, as a pair, cover both the white and the black squares. Their combined strength may be considerably more than twice that of a single Bishop.

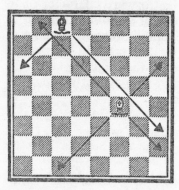

3. Bishop Moves
The arrows indicate the extent of the Bishops' moves. Note that since the Bishops here are situated on opposite-coloured squares, contact between them is impossible. White's Bishop is confined to the black diagonals; Black's to the white diagonals.

The Queen
The modern Queen is far more powerful than the original Minister was in *chaturanga*. Its move combines those of

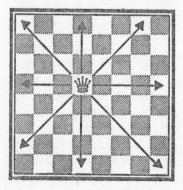

4. Queen Moves
The arrows indicate the extent of the Queen's moves. At the edge of the board the Queen commands 21 squares, but when it is posted in the centre the number is increased by 6 (as with the Bishop) to 27, the maximum for any piece.

the Rook and Bishop. Thus, the Queen moves any number of squares in any given direction (vertically, horizontally or diagonally). The Queen's omnipotence makes it almost the equal of two Rooks.

Capturing

Since the moves of the remaining three men are more varied and complex than those already examined, this is a convenient point to break off and describe how captures are made. Quite apart from its role in checkmate, capturing is as essential to the unfolding of a game of chess as gains and losses are to warfare. The capture and removal of material from the board is the means by which the play progresses from one stage to another, and it is not often that games last many moves without some erosion of the forces. When they do, the outcome is usually a long, attritional trench campaign and perhaps a deadlock at the end of it all.

A capture is effected as follows: instead of being transferred to an empty square, as in the normal way, the capturing piece is moved to the square occupied by the enemy man, which is then taken from the board. Diagram 5 shows some examples of potential Rook, Bishop and Queen captures. When a piece can make a capture that would involve a gain of material or some other, less tangible advantage it is usually said to be 'attacking' or 'threatening' the enemy man; the man threatened in this way is described as being *en prise* (a French term which can be translated as 'liable to be taken').

The diagram on p. 14 also illustrates how the mobility of the long-range pieces tends to be reduced the more men there are present. The white Queen, for instance, cannot reach the squares on the file that are on the other side of the enemy Bishop or those on the long diagonal beyond the Rook. Similarly, the square on which the

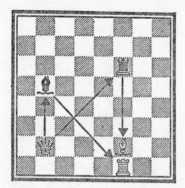

5. Potential Captures
The arrows indicate the four possible captures, two by each side: (i) Queen takes Rook; (ii) Queen takes Bishop; (iii) Black Rook takes Bishop; (iv) Black Bishop takes Rook. Note that the Rooks cannot clash, as the white Bishop is in their way.

white Bishop is standing and the two beyond it on the rank are denied to the Queen. White's Rook is even worse off, since it is confined entirely to squares on the rank: the neighbouring Bishop blocks all access to the file. Rooks, Bishops and Queens need open lines and are therefore seen at their best when captures have cleared some of the material from the board.

The Knight
Unlike the pieces considered so far, the Knight is not able to cover any number of squares in a given direction. Its range is much more limited. The Knight moves directly from one corner of a six-square rectangle (3 x 2) to the diagonally opposite corner, as illustrated in Diagram 6. It cannot stop at any point on the intervening squares but leaps over like the charger it represents (whether or not these squares are occupied by men of either colour makes no difference).

The Knight's range, in addition to being short, depends greatly on where it is situated. In the middle of the board, it can move in 8 directions (as many as the Queen) and so commands 8 squares. At the edge, however, it covers 4 squares at most, while the figure falls to a mere 2 for a

14

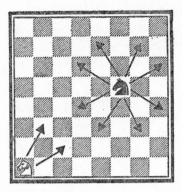

6. Knight Moves
The arrows indicate the imaginary paths of the Knights' moves. Geometrically, they always bisect the Rook's vertical (or horizontal) lines and the Bishop's diagonals. Note that Knight moves starting on white squares finish on black, and *vice versa*.

Knight finding itself in the very corner. In terms of pure mobility it is obvious that the Knight cannot compete with the Rook, Bishop or Queen, but the fact that it is able to jump over the squares adjacent to the one on which it stands gives it an agility all its own. Thanks to this the Knight is far less hampered by the presence of other men and can often penetrate blocked positions when the long-range pieces cannot.

Diagram 7 shows two examples of potential Knight captures. Both demonstrate how the Knight's distinctive qualities may enable it to get the better of more powerful

7. Knight Captures
The arrows indicate the possible captures. In the left-hand half of the diagram the Knight has 'forked' the white Queen and Rook. In the right-hand half the white Knight is attacking a Rook which is shut in and unable to move.

15

pieces. In general, the Knight is considered to be of approximately the same strength as the Bishop. A pair of Bishops, on the other hand, normally outweighs two Knights.

The King

Though the King is the most important piece (its fate settles the game), its range is severely limited. The King moves in any direction (vertically, horizontally or diagonally) but no more than one square at a time, as illustrated in Diagram 8. Its movements are also restricted in another

8. King Moves
The arrows indicate the extent of the King's moves. At the edge of the board the King commands 5 squares instead of its normal 8, while when it is situated in the actual corner the figure is further decreased to 3.

9. A King in Check
The arrow indicates the line of attack by the white Queen. The black King must move out of check, and the only available squares not covered by the Queen or the enemy King are the three on the edge of the board.

respect: it is never permitted to move to a square which is covered by an enemy man. Moreover, when the King is attacked (i.e. threatened with capture) the threat must be parried at once. Such an attack is called a 'check'; this literally means 'king' and is derived (as, too, is 'chess') from the Persian word *shah*.

The King captures in the normal way—subject to the proviso mentioned above. It cannot, therefore, capture an enemy man which is covered (i.e. defended) by another one, since to do so the King would have to submit itself to a check.

10. King Captures
The arrows indicate the possible captures. In the left-hand half of the diagram the King cannot take the Knight because the Bishop defends it. In the right-hand half the black King can get out of check by capturing the Queen.

Owing to the King's special status a valid assessment of its powers is impossible. Inevitably, it is compelled to play a passive role for much of the game, surrounded by a picked bodyguard. When, however, enough captures have occurred to remove the danger of surprise attack, the King may, indeed it should, begin to take a more active part in the proceedings. The King then comes into its own, often excelling the Bishop or Knight in both offensive and defensive actions.

Checkmate

As has been stated, a threat to capture the King must be

parried immediately. If this cannot be done, then it is checkmate (the word is derived from the Persian *shah mat*, meaning 'the King is defeated'). As soon as this indirect capture of the King takes place, the game is over; the player whose King has been mated (mate is the accepted short form for checkmate) has lost.

Diagram 11 shows a straightforward example of mate. A white Rook has been added to the position given in Diagram 9, and as a result Black's King is deprived of retreat squares.

11. Checkmate
Black's King is in check from the Queen and cannot escape. The adjacent squares on the same rank are also attacked by the Queen; the Rook commands the rank to the King's rear; while the squares to its front are covered by the white King.

Checkmate normally follows as a matter of course when one side possesses a big material advantage, but it should not be thought that this is essential. Conditions on the chessboard vary greatly, and it can easily happen that a small force, properly marshalled, will defeat a larger and more powerful one. In Diagram 12, for example, the single white Knight is seen triumphing against all the odds.

Moving the King is not the only method of countering a check. One may also capture the attacker, either with a defending piece or with the King itself (cf. Diagram 10). Furthermore, in the case of a check given by a long-range piece it may be possible to interpose a defender between

18

12. A Smothered Mate
Black's King is in check from the enemy Knight and cannot escape. Here the black Queen, Bishop and Knight contribute to the mate by depriving the King of flight squares. It has been 'smothered' by its own pieces.

the King and its assailant. The black King in Diagram 13 itself has no moves by which to escape the check and it would therefore be mated were it not for the presence of the Bishop. As it is, Black has nothing to fear. Where a check can be parried in several ways it is up to the player, of course, to make the best choice.

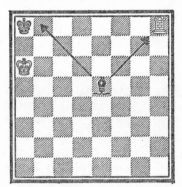

13. Black is not Mated
The arrows indicate the two possible ways that Black has of answering the check. He can either simply capture the Rook, which is *en prise*, or retreat the Bishop to the square next to his King and block the line of attack.

Stalemate
The rules of chess require White and Black to move alternately for the duration of the game, and no exceptions are allowed. However, there is a compromise, as it were,

19

to cover circumstances in which a player (on his turn) is not in check yet at the same time has no legal moves at his disposal. This situation is known as 'stalemate' and brings the game to an immediate conclusion. Neither side is deemed to have won: the result is a draw.

14. Stalemate
Black is unable to move. The three squares within the reach of his King are all controlled by the enemy Queen. But the Queen is not threatening the King at the moment, so there is no question of checkmate.

The position shown in Diagram 14, where White is a full Queen ahead, is a classic example of stalemate. The victory that was apparently within his grasp has been snatched away at the last instant. But appearances can be deceptive in chess, and for that reason stalemate must not be looked on as extraordinary—though curious cases do arise. As a technical device, it plays a very important role in the endgame (the final stage of the game when comparatively few men remain on the board), and many theoretically drawn positions depend upon the inevitability of stalemate with correct play. This will be referred to again later in the book.

Castling

When chess became more dynamic as a result of the reforms made towards the end of the fifteenth century (the powers of the Queen, in particular, were greatly increased) it was found necessary to give further consideration to the

20

15. How to Castle
The arrows indicate how to castle on both the Queen's side (to the left of the broken line) and the King's side (to the right). The King moves two squares towards the Rook in question, which then transfers to the square beyond the King.

security of the King. An effective method was wanted not only of transferring the King to a less exposed spot but also of at the same time improving the co-ordination of the Rooks. A solution was evolved of a combined move by the King and a Rook known as 'castling' (Castle is an alternative name, now rarely used, for the Rook).

Diagram 15 illustrates how castling is carried out. Two points about the operation, as a move, are worth noting: first, it is the only time one may move two pieces simultaneously; second, it is the only time that the King is allowed to move two squares at once. Diagram 16 shows a position in which both players have castled.

16. Castling Completed
White has castled on the Queen's side (referred to simply as castling Queen's side or castling long—from the length of the Rook's move). Black has castled on the King's side (castled King's side or castled short).

The circumstances in which this highly specialised move may be played are strictly limited. To put it negatively, castling is not permitted when any of the following conditions obtain:

(i) Either the King or the Rook in question has previously been moved (it follows that each player can castle but once during the game).

(ii) There is a piece on a square between the King and the Rook (one cannot make a capture when castling).

(iii) The King is in check (whether the Rook is attacked is irrelevant).

(iv) Either the square the King would move to or the square it would cross on the way is covered by an enemy man (the King is not even allowed to move *through* a check).

Only clause (i) represents a permanent disqualification. The others prevent castling while they are applicable and no longer. Also, castling Queen's side and castling King's side are quite independent, and the fact that one is illegal does not necessarily invalidate the other. Diagram 17 will help to clarify all these regulations.

17. Castling Possibilities
White cannot castle because he is in check. If he captures the attacking Knight, he will then be in a position to castle King's side. Black is already able to castle Queen's side (assuming the Rook there and the King have not previously moved).

Although White may eventually be able to castle in the above position, he will certainly never do so on the Queen's side; for he has already moved the Rook. If the Rook were to return to its original square—and this should be noted—, it would not undo what has happened. In that case it would be necessary to *remember* that the Rook had once been moved. Like his opponent, Black still has the right to castle King's side. If he wished to, he would need first to move the obstructing Knight and get rid of the white Bishop (or wait until it is moved) at present commanding the square next to his King.

The situation in Diagram 17 was chosen solely to illustrate the rules that govern castling and is therefore artificial in the extreme. In practical play one would never expect to meet such an unnatural position, with so many pieces yet no pawns.

The Pawn

Pawns are not usually thought of as pieces, unless the word is used in its widest sense. As the foot-soldiers of the chessboard, they form their own division, numerically as strong as the rest and quite distinct from them. The pawn represents the basic unit of force in chess, being even more restricted in its mobility than either the Knight or the King. The pawn normally moves one square forward (or vertically), as illustrated in the left-hand half of Diagram 18. In addition, a pawn that is still on its original square on the second rank (cf. Diagram 1) has the option of advancing either one or two squares, and this is shown in the right-hand half of the diagram.

The most significant aspect of the pawn's move is the fact that it makes no allowance for retreating. All the other men can retire the way they came, but the pawn cannot: every step it takes is permanent. The problem thus raised regarding a pawn's future on reaching the eighth rank (the opponent's first) and being able to advance no further is solved by 'promoting' the pawn. This means that any pawn

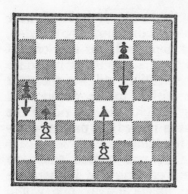

18. Pawn Moves
The arrows indicate the extent of the pawns' moves. The pawns in the left-hand half of the diagram have but one move each. Those in the right-hand half may advance to the third or fourth ranks (counted from each player's side respectively).

that performs the not inconsiderable feat of gaining the opposite side of the board unscathed is immediately transformed into a piece of the same colour (either a Queen, Rook, Bishop or Knight—but *not* a King). The operation of advancing the pawn, removing it from the board and replacing it by a piece is completed in one move. Once the pawn has been moved, therefore, its promotion becomes obligatory (it may never remain on the eighth rank). But the choice of piece to take its place is left to the discretion of the player and is in no sense bound by the material situation at the time. It is theoretically possible for one

19. Pawn Promotion
The arrows indicate the two possible promoting moves. The Knight and Queen on the respective eighth ranks have been promoted from pawns that had completed their journeys, while the other three pieces are present solely to support this statement.

24

side to possess, for instance, ten Bishops. However, a Queen, being the strongest piece, is normally chosen.

There is yet another feature of the pawn's powers that distinguishes it from the pieces. It does not capture in the same way as it moves. The pawn captures diagonally, but only in a forward direction and only one square at a time. This is illustrated in Diagram 20.

20. Pawn Captures
The arrows indicate the possible captures. The pawn in the left-hand half of the diagram is attacking the Knight. In the right-hand half the white pawn on the seventh rank can take either Rook and gain promotion at the same time.

Two further points are worth noting about the above position. One is that White's Bishop is in no danger of being captured at present. While a pawn may start by advancing two squares if the player wishes, the privilege has no connection with capturing. In order to threaten the Bishop the black pawn would first need to move to the third rank, leaving the Knight alone. The second is that the pawns confronting each other on the extreme right of the diagram cannot move at all. This is the fate of all 'blocked' pawns. Unable to capture in a vertical direction, they must remain where they are until either one of them is eliminated or an opportunity occurs to take an enemy man (usually a pawn) on the adjoining file.

En Passant
In the old forms of chess the pawn always moved one

square at a time. When it acquired the right to advance two squares on its first move it was found that in certain circumstances the advantage this conferred was greater than was desirable. The fact was that by moving two squares instead of one a pawn could sometimes by-pass a neighbouring enemy pawn and thus avoid the risk of being captured by it. So a special rule was introduced whereby a pawn could take such a pawn *'en passant'* (French for 'while passing') just as if it had merely advanced to the third rank. This is illustrated in Diagram 21.

21. En Passant Captures
The arrows indicate the possible *en passant* captures. In the left-hand half of the diagram White can equally take either pawn, one normally and one *en passant*. In the right-hand half both black pawns can capture *en passant*.

Taking *en passant* is unique in two respects: first, the pawn which makes the capture (always from the fifth rank) finishes on a different square from that on which the captured pawn stood; second, if a player wishes to make such a capture, he must do so immediately his opponent has advanced the pawn; it cannot be postponed.

The Value of the Men
In order that the exchange of material resulting from captures should as far as possible be profitable the player must be able to value the various chessmen in terms of one another. The simplest method is to take the pawn as common denominator, and this gives the following scale:

pawn—1; Knight—3; Bishop—3; Rook—5; Queen—9. The King is not included, as it cannot be exchanged for other men and is therefore invaluable.

The above set of values is based on mobility and striking-power under average conditions. In particular circumstances totally different figures may apply (a pawn can even prove more effective than a Queen), so one ought always to preserve a flexible outlook. However, exceptional situations tend to be short-lived, and it is generally safe to assume that, for example, three pawns are the approximate equivalent of a Bishop or that two Rooks are worth a Queen and a pawn. With practical experience calculating gains and losses in this way becomes almost automatic.

Finishing a Game

It has already been explained that a game of chess is over as soon as either checkmate or stalemate occurs. But in practice, especially where experts are concerned, these two events hardly ever actually take place. What happens instead is that either one of the players resigns (i.e. admits that his opponent must inevitably enforce checkmate) or both agree to call the game a draw.

In addition to checkmate and stalemate, there is a third fundamental situation which brings the game to an end. This arises when neither side is able to make any effective progress: an equilibrium is reached in which attack and defence are balanced. The result is naturally a draw, but in this case, unlike stalemate, it is difficult to lay down an exact moment when the game must finish; for the number of such positions is astronomical. The rules, therefore, permit the players to agree to a draw at any time within reason. If only the two Kings are left on the board, then obviously nothing further can be achieved, while in positions as level as the one shown in Diagram 22 it is also pointless to continue the struggle. But in more

22. A Typical Draw
White's King, Rook and three pawns are opposed by Black's King, Rook and three pawns, and the deployment of the two forces is practically identical. Each side's defensive position is so strong that it is of no account whose move it is.

complicated situations agreement may not be so easily reached. So, to prevent a game from going on interminably because one side refuses to face facts two special regulations were brought in defining the circumstances in which a drawn outcome must be accepted. These are as follows:

(i) *Repetition of the Position.* The requirement is that the same position (i.e. with pieces of the same kind and colour on the same squares) with the same player to move should occur three times. 'Perpetual check' is the commonest example: thereby the King is exposed to a continuous series of checks which repeat the position without forcing a mate.

(ii) *The 50-Move Rule.* This requires that 50 consecutive moves by each side should occur (at any stage of the game) without a capture taking place or a pawn being moved.

A correct claim by a player that either of the above sets of conditions has been fulfilled immediately finishes the game—it is declared a draw.

Notation
Like mathematics or music, chess has its own forms of notation which enable games to be written down as they

28

are played and kept for future reference. Thanks to this a vast, world-wide literature has been built up based on the achievements of generations of chess masters; the champions of the past live on through the medium of their recorded games.

In English-speaking countries a descriptive system of notation which goes well back into the history of the game still retains its popularity, and this will be used throughout this book. It consists of an abbreviated way of describing the pieces and the squares on the board.

The abbreviations for the pieces are obtained by taking the first letter of their names, thus: King—K; Queen—Q; Rook—R; Bishop—B; Knight—Kt (the last letter is added here to avoid confusion with the King; a single 'N' is also allowed). When it is necessary to differentiate between the respective Rooks, Knights or Bishops a 'K' or 'Q' is prefixed according to whether the piece started the game on the King's side or the Queen's side, e.g. 'KKt' means the King's Knight.

A capital 'P' stands for a pawn, but each pawn also has its own name and abbreviation, derived from the piece on whose file it stands (cf. Diagram 1). The full eight forms are as follows: QRP (Queen's Rook's pawn); QKtP; QBP; QP; KP; KBP; KKtP; KRP. The important thing to note about pawns is that they change their names on making a capture and moving from one file to the next. If a KRP, for example, takes an enemy man, it automatically becomes a KKtP. Pieces, on the other hand, retain their original names throughout the game and no matter where they happen to be situated.

The squares are referred to rather as if they were part of a grid system on a map. Each vertical row (file) receives its name from the piece that starts the game on it, while each horizontal row (rank) is numbered (from 1 to 8) according to its position in relation to the files. A square is named after the file and the rank of which it is a part, and its short form is obtained by using the appropriate piece abbreviation. However, this is not the complete picture. Each square has *two* references, one from White's point of view and one from Black's. This is illustrated in Diagram 23, which gives the abbreviations for every square on the board.

QR1	QKt1	QB1	Q1	K1	KB1	KKt1	KR1
QR8	QKt8	QB8	Q8	K8	KB8	KKt8	KR8
QR2	QKt2	QB2	Q2	K2	KB2	KKt2	KR2
QR7	QKt7	QB7	Q7	K7	KB7	KKt7	KR7
QR3	QKt3	QB3	Q3	K3	KB3	KKt3	KR3
QR6	QKt6	QB6	Q6	K6	KB6	KKt6	KR6
QR4	QKt4	QB4	Q4	K4	KB4	KKt4	KR4
QR5	QKt5	QB5	Q5	K5	KB5	KKt5	KR5
QR5	QKt5	QB5	Q5	K5	KB5	KKt5	KR5
QR4	QKt4	QB4	Q4	K4	KB4	KKt4	KR4
QR6	QKt6	QB6	Q6	K6	KB6	KKt6	KR6
QR3	QKt3	QB3	Q3	K3	KB3	KKt3	KR3
QR7	QKt7	QB7	Q7	K7	KB7	KKt7	KR7
QR2	QKt2	QB2	Q2	K2	KB2	KKt2	KR2
QR8	QKt8	QB8	Q8	K8	KB8	KKt8	KR8
QR1	QKt1	QB1	Q1	K1	KB1	KKt1	KR1

23. Naming the Squares

The lower reference on each square is from White's point of view, the upper from Black's. Thus, the square known as White's QR1 is also known as Black's QR8, while White's QR8 is Black's QR1. The relationship is clear.

To locate a piece or pawn, therefore, one has only to name the square on which it is standing. To go a step further and describe an actual move is a simple matter. A '-' (meaning 'moves to') is used to join up the abbreviations for the piece and the square to which it is moved.

Thus, 'K-K2' would mean that the King moves to the square K2. An 'x' indicates a capture, and in this case the captured piece is named instead of the square. For example, 'KxQ' would mean that the King takes the Queen.

A few other abbreviations and symbols are also used: 'ch' for check; 'O-O' for castling King's side; 'O-O-O' for castling Queen's side; '=' for pawn promotion; 'e.p.' for *en passant*.

There are two basic methods of laying out moves in written form: either in columns, one for White's moves and one for Black's; or running on like a sentence. Both methods are frequently used at the same time; for whereas the first is ideal for recording the text of a game, only the second is suitable for inclusion in a commentary. Moves are usually numbered, and where they run on one after the other some form of puncuation is normal, though it is not obligatory.

A Complete Game
This introductory chapter has dealt with the rudiments of chess and its mechanics. To round it off and perhaps whet the reader's appetite, here is a complete game—and a celebrated one. It was won by Paul Morphy, the American chess genius, against two opponents in consultation, the Duke of Brunswick and Count Isouard, and took place in a box at the Paris Opera in 1858 during a performance of *The Barber of Seville*. Morphy was White.

White	Black	White	Black
1 P-K4	P-K4	5 QxB	PxP
2 Kt-KB3	P-Q3	6 B-QB4	Kt-KB3
3 P-Q4	B-Kt5	7 Q-QKt3	Q-K2
4 PxP	BxKt	8 Kt-B3	P-B3

9 B-KKt5	P-Kt4	14 R-Q1	Q-K3
10 KtxP	PxKt	15 BxR ch	KtxB
11 BxKtP ch	QKt-Q2	16 Q-Kt8 ch	KtxQ
12 O-O-O	R-Q1	17 R-Q8 mate	
13 RxKt	RxR		

Two points should be noticed about how the notation is used in this game score. First, White's moves are always described from White's point of view and Black's moves from Black's point of view. Second, the full abbreviation of a piece or square is only necessary to avoid ambiguity. Thus, 1 P-K4 is perfectly clear, for the KP alone can move to K4 in the initial position; similarly, 3 . . . , B-Kt5 (this is the normal way of denoting a Black move when it stands alone) cannot be misinterpreted, as only one black Bishop can move to one of the Kt5 squares. Fluency comes with practice.

2

ELEMENTARY ENDINGS

To play a game of chess it is only necessary to know what the object is (checkmate) and how the pieces move. But it is one thing to play chess, another to understand it. Morphy understood the principles of chess better than any of his contemporaries, and this showed itself in the way that he was able to defeat them. The player's task, therefore, is to learn not so much what moves to make but rather the reasons for them.

At the beginning of the game the forces on each side are equal in strength and drawn up directly opposite each other. This fact raises an important question: How can a player legitimately expect to fulfil the object of the game? The answer is that he cannot. Chess theory assumes that it is impossible for either side to mate the other if both play correctly and that a draw is the logical result. It is not as simple in practice, however, for in the majority of cases the definition of 'correct' depends on judgment, which in its turn stems from knowledge, skill and experience. Chess is not an exact science, and it is the relative abilities of the two contestants that finally count.

Since White always starts the game by making the first move, he enjoys the initiative in the early stages—he can dictate matters to some extent. The plans on both sides develop accordingly: White aims to increase his initiative and transform it into a permanent advantage, while Black aims to neutralise it and, if possible, obtain counterplay. But what constitutes a significant advantage? When is it enough to win? The answers to these questions are not to be found by studying the initial position or any other position where there are still a large number of men on the board. They are far too complicated. The problem is best tackled by going straight to the endgame and seeing just what determines the basic theory of won and drawn games.

If all the men have been captured or exchanged and the Kings alone remain, the result is an automatic draw. That is fundamental. But when an additional man is left on the board, it is a different matter. The point then to be decided is whether the stronger side (conventionally always White in constructed examples) can exploit the material advantage and mate the opponent. This is possible in the case of a Queen or Rook but not a Bishop or Knight.

Mate with a Queen

The ending of King and Queen versus King represents the winning process in its most elementary form. The method is simple: the lone King is driven to the edge of the board, where it runs out of retreat squares and is unable to avoid being mated. From the position in Diagram 24 this can be accomplished as follows:

24. Basic Mating Technique
The black King can neither be mated in the middle of the board nor by the Queen alone. It must first be restricted in its movements and confined to the edge; then it is mated by the white Queen in co-operation with the King.

1 Q-Q3, K-B3; 2 Q-B4 ch, K-Kt3; 3 K-Q7, K-Kt2; 4 Q-Kt5 ch, K-R2; 5 K-B7, K-R1; 6 Q-R6 mate.

The great power of the Queen makes it very easy to overcome the enemy King's efforts to stay in the safety of the middle of the board. On the other hand, it also involves the risk of stalemate; for a King in the corner can be completely deprived of moves by a Queen (cf. Diagram 14). When the King has been confined to the edge, therefore, it is wise to leave it two free squares on which to mark time until mate is possible. That avoids all danger of a draw by accidental stalemate.

Mate with a Rook
The ending of King and Rook versus King poses the stronger side more problems, since the Rook is by no means as powerful as the Queen. It cannot drive the enemy King to the edge of the board single-handed but must rely from the start on the co-operation of the King. Essentially, however, the winning process of restriction of the King's movements is the same.

25. Rook-Mate Technique
The black King is already restricted to the KB, KKt, and KR files. White's King and Rook must work together to drive it back and confine it to the edge of the board, after which mate will be unavoidable.

From the position in Diagram 25 play could proceed as follows: **1 K-Q3, K-B4; 2 K-Q4, K-B3; 3 R-K5, K-Kt3; 4 K-Q5, K-B3; 5 K-Q6, K-B2; 6 R-B5 ch, K-Kt3; 7 K-K6, K-Kt2; 8 R-Kt5 ch, K-R3; 9 K-B6, K-R2; 10 R-R5 ch, K-Kt1; 11 R-R4, K-B1; 12 R-R8 mate.** As a general rule,

35

it takes a Rook about twice as many moves as a Queen to force mate.

The Minor Pieces

The terms 'major piece' and 'minor piece' are in regular use to distinguish the Queen and Rook on the one hand from the Bishop and Knight on the other. They are justified purely on the grounds of the difference in general striking-power, but they also hold good in a more particular respect: a major piece (supported by the King) can force mate—as we have just seen—against the lone King, whereas a minor piece cannot. Neither a Bishop nor a Knight commands adjoining squares on the same file or rank, which the geometry of the chessboard requires of a piece in such circumstances.

26. Stalemate with a Bishop
Even if the lone King is restricted to one square, there is no danger. Were it White's move, he could not improve his position; mate is impossible.

27. Stalemate with a Knight
Here too it is of no significance whether the black King is in the centre of the board or the corner. There is no mate.

Diagrams 26 and 27 illustrate the worst than can happen to the weaker side in an ending of King and minor piece versus King. A draw is the only possible result.

King and Pawn versus King

Like the minor pieces, the pawn is not strong enough,

even with the support of the King, actually to mate the lone King. Stalemate, as shown in Diagram 28, is again the most that can be achieved.

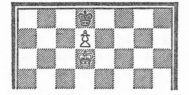

28. Stalemate with a Pawn
It is Black's move and his King has been stalemated. The same sort of draw may occur on any file.

However, a pawn does not have to remain a pawn. Its potential strength is far greater than a minor piece's, for it can become a Queen on reaching the eighth rank. The outcome of the ending of King and pawn versus King therefore depends on whether or not the pawn can be successfully promoted. If it can, the stronger side wins; if not, the game is drawn.

There are basically two types of situation to be considered. In one the pawn has to seek promotion unaided; in the other it is supported by the King. The first case is illustrated in Diagram 29, where White's King is clearly too far away to give any help. The decisive question is whether the black King can get across the board in time

29. Entering the 'Square'
The thick line indicates the 'square of the pawn.' If it is Black's move, he can put his King 'in the square' by playing it either to K4 or K5. If it is White's move, the pawn can advance out of the opponent's reach.

to reach the pawn, and in answering this the so-called 'rule of the square' comes in useful. It enables the player to see in an instant what the pawn's prospects of promotion are and thus saves tedious calculations. Wherever the defending King is situated within the 'square of the pawn' it is certain of being able to catch the pawn.

In the rare event of the pawn's still being on the second rank allowance must be made for the fact that it can advance two squares on its first move; the 'square of the pawn' would then be the same as if the pawn were already on the third rank. For instance, if the pawn in the above example were on QR2, the 'square of the pawn' would cover White's QR3, KB3, KB8 and QR8. The black King would again be 'in the square', and the game would be drawn as follows: 1 P-R4 (reaching the position in Diagram 29), K-K5; 2 P-R5, K-Q4; 3 P-R6, K-B3; 4 P-R7, K-Kt2; 5 P-R8=Q ch, KxQ.

The second type of situation is more complex. In general, the weaker side can hope to draw against a supported pawn only if the King can occupy a square in its path (e.g. as in Diagram 28). Diagram 30 shows a position where the black King had been unable to get to the squares in front of the pawn and as a result is powerless to prevent it from becoming a Queen. The one exception is the case

30. The Pawn cannot be Stopped

The white King controls both the squares in front of the pawn, thus guaranteeing its promotion. White will win by K-R7 followed by P-Kt7 and P-Kt8=Q.

of a RP, as illustrated in Diagram 31. With his King on the edge of the board, White is very much more restricted in his movements and must be content with a draw after 1 K-R8, K-B1; 2 P-R7, K-B2 stalemate. If it is Black's

31. The Weakness of a RP
Here the white King has but one way (the Kt file) that it can take to allow the pawn through, compared with two for the other pawns.

move he draws by **1 . . . , K-B1; 2 K-Kt6, K-Kt1; 3 P-R7 ch, K-R1; 4 K-R6** stalemate (cf. Diagram 28). Naturally, had the black King been farther away—say, at Q2—then White (to move) could have won by **1 K-Kt7**. The B1 and B2 squares are the key ones for the defender: if his King can reach one of them in time, the game is drawn.

When the defending King is able to occupy a square in the path of the pawn it is obvious that the result will be a draw if the stronger side does not succeed in forcing the King to give way. The lack of room at the edge of the board makes this task impossible with a RP, but in the case of the other pawns success depends upon the position of the white King. The ideal situation is shown in Diagram 32. White's King has reached the sixth rank ahead of the pawn and is now ready to drive the enemy King away from the queening square. If it is Black's move, he loses at once by, for example, **1 . . . , K-K1; 2 K-B7, K-K2; 3 P-Q6 ch**—the pawn's promotion is assured. If it is White's turn, he wins as follows: **1 K-K6** (1 K-B6 is equally good), **K-K1; 2 P-Q6, K-Q1; 3 P-Q7, K-B2; 4 K-K7,** and again the pawn queens.

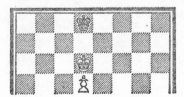

32. Ideal for White
White wins all such positions except those with a RP. Here his King may also be on QB6 or K6.

On the other hand, it is ideal for Black if the White King stands behind the pawn, as was seen in Diagram 28. Such positions are drawn—except when the pawn (but not a RP) is on the seventh rank and it is White's move. Thus from the position shown in Diagram 33 play could

33. Ideal for Black
The pawn is blockaded. No matter who moves first, Black is forced to retreat step by step. The same type of position occurs with the pawn on each successive rank, until Black finally runs out of squares and is stalemated.

continue: 1 K-K3, K-Q3; 2 K-K4, K-K3; 3 P-Q5 ch, K-Q3; 4 K-Q4, K-Q2; 5 K-K5, K-K2; 6 P-Q6 ch, K-Q2; 7 K-Q5, K-Q1; 8 K-K6, K-K1; 9 P-Q7 ch, K-Q1; 10 K-Q6 stalemate (Diagram 28 again).

Between these two ideals, where the outcome is clear, there is a third, most critical type of position, in which the result rests upon whose turn it is to move. Diagram 34 is an example. The white King is better placed than in Diagram 33, being in front of the pawn, but has not yet reached the sixth rank, as it had in Diagram 32. This makes all the difference, for now the defending King has more space in which to manoeuvre. Thus after 1 K-K5, K-K2; 2 P-Q5, K-Q2; 3 P-Q6 it is not squeezed out but can maintain the blockade of the pawn by 3 . . . , K-Q1, when Black draws as above (4 K-K6, K-K1 etc.). However, if it is Black's turn to move, he is forced to let the white King through at once, e.g. 1 . . . , K-K2; 2 K-B6, K-Q1; 3 K-Q6, and White has achieved his objective.

34. Result in Balance
The question is whether White can establish the ideal winning position. If it is his move, his King's advance is blocked by the black King and it is a draw. If it is Black's move, he must give way and is therefore lost.

The striking feature of the above position is the fact that both sides find having to move a disadvantage—it even costs Black the game. This apparent paradox (in general, the initiative of the move is not to be turned down) plays an important part in pawn endings, particularly those which develop into a duel between the Kings. When the Kings oppose each other as they do in Diagram 34, they are described as being 'in opposition'. The one which has to move must give way to the other, which is said to 'have the opposition'. The 'opposition' is therefore a valuable weapon, and the struggle to obtain it and keep it is often decisive. Diagram 35 shows a position where application of the principle of the opposition enables the correct move to be found at once and an insidious trap avoided. White gets nowhere by advancing the pawn, as the black King is inside the 'square'. If he is to win, he must get his King to the Q file and then force Black to give way. But after the obvious 1 K-Kt5, K-Kt2; 2 K-B5, K-B2; 3 K-K5, K-K2; 4 K-Q5, K-Q2 the position in Diagram 34 is reached with White to move and it is a draw. The right plan is 1 K-R5, K-Kt2; 2 K-Kt5, K-B2; 3 K-B5, K-K2; 4 K-K5, K-Q2; 5 K-Q5. Now it is Black's move, and that loses him the game.

35. Use of the Opposition
At present. neither King has the opposition, since there are two squares between them instead of one. It is White's move, and he wins by taking the opposition on the R file and keeping it as the Kings move across to the centre.

The opposition can also occur on the rank or diagonal and at a distance (i.e. with either three or five squares between the Kings). In the position in Diagram 36 Black is better placed than in the previous example, despite the fact that his King is back in the very corner. The point is that Black can maintain the opposition if it is White's move, yet White cannot if it is Black's. After **1 K-Kt4** (1 K-R5 and 1 K-Kt5 are answered by 1 . . . , K-R2 and 1 . . . , K-Kt2 respectively),**K-Kt1** (Black loses the opposition if he plays his King to the second rank); **2 K-B4, K-B1; 3 K-K4, K-K1; 4 K-K5, K-K2** Black draws as before. With Black to move, the continuation is as

36. Distant Opposition
There is no difference in principle between distant and normal opposition. They are often interchangeable, and here the effect is the same as if the black King were on KR3: it is a draw, whoever is to move.

42

follows: **1 . . . , K-Kt1; 2 K-Kt4, K-B1; 3 K-B4, K-K1; 4 K-K4, K-Q1,** and the white King is forced on to the fifth rank by the pawn, thus losing the opposition.

If the stronger side's King is two squares in front of the pawn, the game is won (except in the case of a RP) regardless of who has the opposition. This is because, as shown in Diagram 37, there is a pawn move in reserve

37. Reserve Pawn Move
If White has the opposition, Black must give way at once. If Black has the opposition, White can stand fast with his King and expend his reserve pawn move, after which the black King is again at a loss.

which can be used should it be necessary. Thus, **1 P-Q4** gives White the opposition (Diagram 34) and enables him to win easily.

To sum up, the ending of King and pawn versus King is essentially a struggle between the Kings for key squares in relation to the pawn. The stronger side's general aim is to obtain the opposition and reach the sixth rank with his King in front of the pawn; the defending side seeks to prevent this and to force the pawn to advance before the King.

Mate with Two Bishops

If the advantage of one extra man is frequently sufficient to win, one might expect that the addition of another would always be decisive. However, that is not the case. Apart from the examples of draws involving pawns, there are

even those where two minor pieces cannot force mate.
Two Bishops operating on the same-coloured squares (one
the result of pawn promotion) are no more effective, for
instance, than a single Bishop. The lone King is quite
safe on squares of the opposite colour; the worst that can
happen to it is stalemate, as illustrated in Diagram 38.

**38. Stalemate with Two
'Blind' Bishops**
These two Bishops can follow
each other about on the black
squares, but the world of the
white squares is forever closed
to them. Mate is impossible.

When the two Bishops are a genuine pair (i.e. one is
'white-squared' and the other 'black-squared') it is a
different story. Together they sweep the board and leave
the enemy King no hope of escape. The winning process
consists, as in the Queen and Rook mates, in restricting
the King to the edge, though here the mate cannot be
forced until the King has been driven into the corner.
From the position in Diagram 39 play could continue as

39. Commanding Bishops
Two Bishops are exceptionally
powerful when centrally placed
like this. The black King cannot approach them and is
already confined to a small
sector of the board. To re-
strict it further White's King
must be brought into action.

follows: **1 K-B4, K-Q3; 2 K-B5, K-K2; 3 B-K5, K-Q2;
4 K-B6, K-B1; 5 K-K6** (but not 5 K-K7 stalemate)**, K-Q1;**

6 B-QKt7, K-K1; 7 B-B7, K-B1; 8 K-B6, K-K1; 9 B-B6 ch, K-B1; 10 B-Q6 ch, K-Kt1; 11 K-Kt6, K-R1; 12 B-Q7 (this waiting move sets the stage for the mate), K-Kt1; 13 B-K6 ch, K-R1; 14 B-K5 mate. A point worth noting is that the white King should aim for one of the squares a Knight's move away from the corner where the mate takes place. The two Bishops usually require a move or so more than a Rook to mate.

Mate with Two Knights

It was stated earlier that a pair of Bishops normally outweighs two Knights. There is no better proof of this than the fact that the Knights are unable to force mate against the lone King. The word 'force' is significant, for mate can occur if the weaker side defends himself inaccurately. This is illustrated in Diagram 40.

40. Black Draws with Correct Play
If White checks at B6, Black must not move his King into the corner because of Kt-B7 mate. Instead, the correct . . . , K-B1 leaves him perfectly safe.

In the above position the black King can avoid the dangerous R1 square. It cannot always do so, however; for if White deploys his Knights differently, he can compel

41. Cornered but Stalemated
Further progress is impossible because the Knight which prevented the black King's escape via QB1 when it was checked cannot reach the mating square (QB7) in one move.

45

the King to fall back to the corner. But then, as shown in Diagram 41, the problem of stalemate arises. Since this is not to be overcome, the ending of King and two Knights versus King is a theoretical draw.

Mate with Bishop and Knight

The partnership of Bishop and Knight lies in terms of strength somewhere between those of the two Bishops and two Knights. The lone King can be mated by force, but the process may take twice as long as it would with the Bishop pair. It is again necessary to confine the King to the corner, but in this case there is an additional requirement: the corner square must be of the colour that the Bishop controls.

The winning method may be divided into three separate stages: first, the King is driven into a 'safe' corner (it will steer clear of the others when retreating); second, it is forced across to one of the 'right' corners; there, finally, it is mated. For practical reasons these are best studied in reverse order.

Diagram 42 shows a position where the black King is

42. White Poised to Finish the Mate
Note how the white pieces co-operate to imprison the enemy King. From here they need six moves to close in and administer the mate.

already restricted to four squares in one of the mating corners. This represents the objective of the second stage of the plan. White finishes his task as follows: **1 B-R6, K-R2; 2 B-B8, K-Kt1; 3 Kt-Kt4, K-R2; 4 K-B7, K-R1; 5 B-Kt7 ch, K-R2; 6 Kt-B6 mate.**

The sort of position in which the second stage starts is illustrated in Diagram 43. It takes fourteen moves to

43. Black King in a 'Safe' Corner

It is impossible for the black King to be mated where it is, for the Bishop does not control the corner square. But Black's safety is short-lived.

drive the black King out of its cover and across the board to the position in Diagram 42. Play proceeds: **1 Kt-B7 ch, K-Kt1; 2 B-Kt6, K-B1; 3 B-R7, K-K1; 4 Kt-K5, K-Q1;** (or **4 . . . , K-B1; 5 Kt-Q7 ch, K-K1; 6 K-K6, K-Q1; 7 B-Q3, K-K1; 8 B-Kt5, K-Q1; 9 Kt-B6, K-B2; 10 Kt-Q5 ch,** transposing into the main line); **5 K-K6, K-B2; 6 Kt-Q7, K-Kt2; 7 B-Q3, K-B3; 8 B-R6, K-B2; 9 B-Kt5, K-Q1; 10 Kt-Kt6, K-B2; 11 Kt-Q5 ch, K-Q1; 12 K-Q6, K-B1; 13 K-K7, K-Kt2; 14 K-Q7, K-Kt1.**

Cornering the lone King in the first place is simple enough, as it dare not stray too far towards the mating corners for fear of being trapped at once. From the position shown in Diagram 44 the continuation could be: **1 B-Q3, K-B3; 2 K-Q5, K-B2; 3 K-K5, K-K2; 4 B-B5, K-B2; 5 Kt-K3, K-Kt2; 6 K-K6, K-Kt1; 7 K-B6, K-R1; 8 Kt-B4, K-Kt1; 9 Kt-K5, K-R1,** and the initial stage of the mating process is completed (Diagram 43).

44. Cornering the King

The technique is to use mainly the King and Bishop to push Black back, keeping the Knight in the background. Being unable to maintain a stand near the centre, the black King must retreat towards the KR1 corner, where it is temporarily safe.

Although the ending of King, Bishop and Knight versus King is exceedingly rare in practice, its value as an exercise is considerable. It may be said to represent in an elementary form much of what is essential to the chess struggle. To exploit his material superiority the stronger side must pursue a logical campaign aimed at the gradual conquest of the board and the reduction of the enemy King's manœuvring space. Beginners are advised to play out this ending just as if it were a full-scale game, starting with the pieces in various positions. This will help to develop the ability to co-ordinate one's forces, plan ahead and calculate particular lines. If 50 moves elapse before the lone King is mated, then the result is a draw under the 50-Move Rule. A reasonable attention to accuracy will thus be encouraged from the start.

3

TACTICAL ELEMENTS

For the balance of power on the board to be materially disturbed—which, in general, is what decides whether one side has an advantage that will eventually be sufficient for mate—it is necessary for the two armies to engage each other in action and for casualties to be sustained. An action in chess invariably comes under the heading of 'tactics' and may be far-ranging in scope: from ordinary captures and exchanges to difficult sacrificial combinations, on the one hand, and from simple threats to lengthy manœuvres designed to weaken the enemy position, on the other. All such operations, no matter how complicated, can be broken down to their elements, and these a chessplayer can recognise and learn to apply just as a mathematician can formulae or a musician chords.

Attack and Defence
No clash of forces can take place without the element of attack being involved: the initiative must stem from one side or the other. Defence is a different matter: it may take the form of a counter-attack or flight or even be non-existent. The last is often the case in games between beginners, who may go as far as not to realise at all that a man is threatened. The result is that the opponent captures it for nothing.

If attack and defence are evenly balanced, then the aggressor will be unable to win material by capturing. Such a situation is illustrated in Diagram 45, where White achieves no more than an exchange of Rooks by 1 RxR,

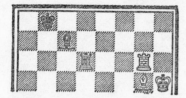

45. Adequate Defence
Black's Rook is protected by the Bishop. As attack and defence cancel each other, the chances are level.

BxR. But suppose we add a white Rook at KR6 and a black Rook at QKt2, which gives us the position in Diagram 46. Now White finishes a piece up after **1 RxR, BxR; 2 RxB.**

46. Inadequate Defence
Here Black's Rook, still covered by the Bishop, is twice attacked. The defence is therefore outnumbered.

When the piece that is threatened is of greater value than its attacker, then it is not enough to protect it. In Diagram 47, for example, the continuation **1 BxR, PxB** represents a definite success for White. The gain of a

47. White Wins Material
Though Black's Rook is protected by the pawn, that does not save its life. Rooks are worth more than Bishops.

Rook for a minor piece like this is called 'winning the exchange'; accordingly, 'the exchange' (as distinct from *an* exchange, e.g. Rook for Rook or Queen for Queen) has come to be the measure of the difference between a Rook and a Bishop or Knight. The only course for the more valuable piece is to take evasive action.

50

Conversely, if it is the attackers that are worth more, then it is not important whether the defence is outnumbered. In the position in Diagram 48 White can

48. White cannot Win Material
While the Knight is attacked twice and defended only once, its capture would cost White one of his Rooks.

eliminate two enemy men for one of his own by **1 RxKt, PxR; 2 RxP,** but in doing so he loses the exchange for a pawn. The attack on the Knight is therefore lacking in bite; the defence is on top.

Double Attack
Since the defender can parry most simple threats by either bringing up reserves or judiciously retreating the attacked piece, more forceful methods of seeking an advantage are required. The 'double attack' (often called the 'fork') certainly meets the need. In this, as the name implies, one man attacks two of the opponent's simultaneously, thus facing him with the unpleasant choice of which one to save. If a check is involved, as in Diagram 49, the defender

49. Double Attack on King and Rook
The 'forking' action of the white Queen must result in material gain. Black is obliged to move his King out of check and abandon the Rook.

does not have even this option, for the safety of the King comes before everything else.

All the pieces can carry out double attacks, though the Queen is obviously the best-equipped for the purpose.

The Rook frequently finds its victims in undefended minor pieces on a rank, as illustrated in Diagram 50. One of them is bound to fall.

50. Helpless Minor Pieces
The Rook threatens the Bishop and the Knight at the same time. Neither can save its colleague by protecting it.

If the Bishops and Knights are helpless against the horizontal and vertical attacks of the major pieces, they also have their opportunities to hit back. And when they do the more valuable pieces cannot rely on mutual protection. Thus in Diagram 51 the Rooks are powerless to

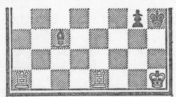

51. Bishop Attacking Rooks
The Rooks have been caught in the Bishop's diagonal fire. It is clear that both cannot escape unscathed.

prevent the Bishop from taking one of them. Diagram 52 shows a Knight delivering a deadly blow, attacking not only Queen and Rook but the King as well. It costs Black his Queen.

52. A 'Family' Fork
The Knight specialises in many-pronged assaults, exploiting the fact that its mode of action is peculiar to itself.

The pawns are very slow footed compared with the pieces, but for all that they enjoy their share of double attacks. Two examples are illustrated in Diagram 53. In such situations it is the minor pieces that have to bite the dust; that is bad enough, but the loss of a Rook or Queen for a pawn—even two or three—is normally so crippling that it is useless to continue the struggle.

53. Typical Pawn Forks
In the left-hand half of the diagram the pawn has got under the guard of the Rook and Knight. In the right-hand half the Bishop can hit back and take the KtP, but White would recapture with his RP and win material.

It is rarely possible for the King to take an active part in tactical operations before the endgame is reached. At that stage, when the open board conceals fewer hazards, it is able to compete on more or less level terms with the other pieces (except the all-powerful Queen). As Diagram 54 shows, if the King gets to close quarters with the

54. Attacking Kings
Rooks are vulnerable diagonally; Bishops vertically and horizontally; Knights from all angles; pawns from directly in front, laterally and from behind. Here these weaknesses have been exploited and both Kings have the opposing forces at their mercy.

enemy, it can prove a formidable weapon and well capable of executing double attacks.

Discovered Attack

As long as the players are wary, there are few occasions when one piece is so favourably placed that it can successfully attack two of the enemy at once. However, that is not the only way that simultaneous threats may arise. An alternative method is to move one man into a threatening position and by doing so to 'discover' an attack by a second piece in another direction. This is illustrated in Diagram 55. The exact sequence would be **1 B-R7 ch, KxB; 2 QxQ,** and White has won a Queen for a Bishop. The minor piece sacrifices itself willingly.

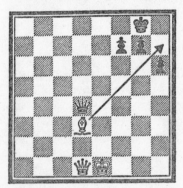

55. Discovered Attack
White can threaten King and Queen at one stroke by moving his Bishop as indicated by the arrow. This gives check and also clears the Q file. Black must then safeguard his King, leaving the Queen to be taken on White's next move.

If the piece that is unmasked does the checking, then the term 'discovered check' is used. A situation comparable with the previous example is shown in Diagram 56. After **1 B-Kt7 ch, K-Q1; 2 BxQ, KxB** the result is the same.

By the nature of things, a discovered attack can only come from a long-range piece, but there is nothing to prevent a Knight, pawn or even the King from doing the unmasking. In Diagram 57 it is a pawn: White plays

56. Discovered Check
By moving his Bishop as indicated by the arrow White again threatens King and Queen simultaneously. The clearing of the K file forces the enemy King to take cover, which in turn allows White the time to win the Queen.

57. Discovered Attack along a Diagonal
The advance of the BP will threaten the Knight and open the diagonal for the Bishop to attack the enemy Rook. Black cannot save both pieces.

1 P-B7, winning at least a piece. In Diagram 58 it is a King move that decides the issue: by **1 K-B6** White takes advantage of the fact that the black pieces are split up and unable to defend one another. Such lack of co-operation is always an invitation to the attacker.

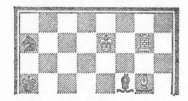

58. Clearing a Rank
White can move his King so as to threaten the Bishop and clear the seventh rank for his Rook.

The Pin

If a man cannot move out of the line of fire of an enemy piece without exposing a colleague to attack, it is said to be 'pinned'. A simple example is shown in Diagram 59. This type of pin is complete in its effect. Others vary

59. A Rook Pinned by a Bishop
Black is unable to move his Rook out of the way of the Bishop because his King is behind it on the same diagonal and requires protection.

in the extent to which they limit the mobility of the pinned man. The black Queen in Diagram 60, for instance, is not entirely deprived of moves: it does not have to wait helplessly where it is until it is taken for nothing. This is because the Queen's powers enable it to match anything undertaken by the Rook.

60. A Pinned Queen
Black's Queen is pinned against his King by the enemy Rook. While it may not seek to escape to the right or left, it still has the run of the K file and can either capture the Rook or retreat to a safer square.

A pinned piece is only compelled to remain under attack if it protects the King. In other cases it is free to move away and leave its colleague to look after itself. Thus, in the position in Diagram 61 Black must resign himself to the loss of the exchange after 1 . . . , Kt-K2; 2 BxR, KxB. That is better than losing the Knight without compensation.

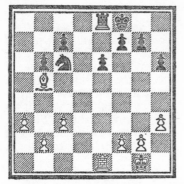

61. Moving a Pinned Piece
Black's ·Knight is pinned against his Rook by the enemy Bishop and is under threat of immediate capture. As it cannot be protected, Black has no choice but to move the Knight and let the Rook, which is defended, be taken.

Most of the pins that occur in practice are not as drastic as those given above. The pinned man can usually rely on sufficient support to meet the opponent's direct threats, and consequently the critical question is whether or not the pressure can be increased. The following two examples illustrate ways in which this may be achieved. In Diagram 62 White obtains a winning material advantage at once

62. A Winning Pawn Thrust
Black's pinned Knight is adequately protected against the Bishop's attack. However, being unable to leave its post, it offers the white pawns a sitting target. All that White has to do is thrust forward his KKtP and win a piece.

by **1 P-Kt5, PxP; 2 PxP, K-B1; 3 PxKt.** The situation shown in Diagram 63 is rather more complicated, but again White can win a piece by a forced series of moves: **1 Kt-K5, R-Q3; 2 KtxKt, BxKt; 3 Q-B3, Q-Q2; 4 BxB,**

57

63. Strengthening a Pin
The black Knight, pinned against the Queen by the enemy Rook, is secure for the moment. But White can immediately increase the pressure by threatening it with his Knight and Bishop. Finally, the Queen can be brought in to break Black's resistance.

and Black cannot recapture the Bishop without losing his Rook. It should be noted how the pin on the QB file immobilises first Black's Knight and then his Bishop, thereby allowing White time to throw in more attackers.

One normally thinks of a pinned piece as being of less value than the one behind it. However, as Diagram 64

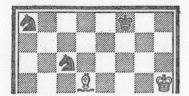

64. Defenceless Knights
The Knights have been caught off guard, that on QB3 being pinned against the other. One of them must fall.

makes clear, this is not necessarily so. The word 'skewer' is often used to describe pins of this sort, and the term seems even more fitting when the attacked piece outweighs the one behind it. Little can be done then but retreat the more valuable man and permit the skewer to take its full effect. When the King is involved, there is of course no option at all. Thus in Diagram 65 Black is helpless, finishing a Rook down after **1 . . . , K-K3; 2 RxR.**

Like discovered attacks, pins of all forms are based on the operations of the long-range pieces. In fact, the two

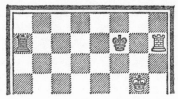

65. A Winning Skewer
Black must move his King out of check and leave his Rook to be taken by his opponent's for nothing.

devices are closely related. In both two men oppose each other directly (on a rank, file or diagonal) with a third between them. If this third piece is active, then moving it usually results in a discovered attack; if it is passive, it is because it is pinned.

Tactical Patterns
Skill in the field of tactics depends greatly on the ability to recognise the patterns that the forces weave in their encounters on the chessboard. When a player detects the existence of simple geometric relationships between the various positions of the pieces both before and in the course of a possible action he should look carefully for a tactical idea that may provide the link. In many cases it can be turned to his advantage.

In the position in Diagram 66 White's pieces have been forked by the black Queen and are unable to protect one

66. Resourceful Minor Pieces
White can save the day by exploiting the fact that the enemy King and Queen are lined up on a diagonal which the Bishop is able to control. It pins the Queen, which exposes itself to a Knight fork if it captures the Bishop.

another by direct means (e.g. 1 Kt-Kt4 would be defeated by 1 . . . , Q-B6 ch). But they can do so indirectly—by counter-attacking. Thus, after **1 B-Kt5, QxB; 2 Kt-B7 ch, K-Q2; 3 KtxQ** the result is a draw. Two tactical elements are co-ordinated here in one operation, and each is reflected in the pattern shown in Diagram 67. The

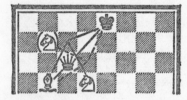

67. Pin and Fork Pattern
The forking action of the Knight on QKt7 (bracketed) is indicated by the broken lines; it balances the design.

alternative placing of the Knight at QKt7 instead of Q5 emphasises the logical nature of the situation and the way White's manœuvre works.

It is easy to see that the above plan could also be carried out with the Knight on a number of other squares. To get a complete picture it is necessary to move the actors nearer to the centre of the board, as in Diagram 68 (that

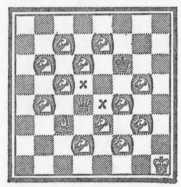

68. Tactical Pattern in Full
Each bracketed Knight stands for an alternative placing; there are thus twelve in all. The squares marked with a cross are those on which the fork occurs (depending on where the Knight comes from) after the capture of the Bishop.

the action now takes place on different-coloured squares is of no significance). The impressive feature of the design is its symmetry. The interplay of forces, represented by the pieces, leads to set formations; there are no irregularities.

Practically speaking, no limit can be put to the number of such tactical patterns. They range from simple lines and angles to complex figures made up of differing shapes. However, detailed knowledge is not of much use; the important thing is to appreciate how the ideas fit together; for that gives a player the 'feel' for tactics so essential for success.

4

STRATEGIC ELEMENTS

Whereas tactics means action and material exchanges, strategy refers to the methods of preparing the ground for such operations. To be worthy of his command, a general must be able to deploy his army effectively, to recognise the strengths and weaknesses of a position and to work out an appropriate plan of campaign. The better he fulfils these tasks the more likely it is that tactical clashes, whenever and wherever they arise, will turn out in his favour.

In contrast to tactics, which is essentially dynamic, chess strategy is founded on the static features of the position. These are composed principally of three elements: the terrain itself (the board); the pawn formation; and the location of the Kings. The other pieces, being free agents and far more mobile, tend to have an intermittent or fleeting effect on the choice of plan.

The Centre

In the elementary endings an advantage in space proves to be as necessary for final victory as the extra material. Even in the case of King and Queen versus King mate is impossible before the lone King has been driven to the edge of the board, for it is only then that the number of flight squares is sufficiently reduced. The stronger side therefore first gains control of the central squares (see Diagram 69) and proceeds from there to a domination of the board as a whole.

The conquest of the centre as a strategic objective is

69. Central Squares
The expression 'the centre' usually refers to the four squares in the middle of the board, bounded here by the thick line. But in a general sense the larger area within the broken line is also described as the centre.

equally important in all phases of the game. Pieces that are centrally placed can operate almost anywhere at a moment's notice, while those that lurk in the rear or to one side need time to get themselves organised for an action which is not in their vicinity. In other words, centralisation brings with it increased manœuvrability and effectiveness.

The player who has got the upper hand in the struggle for the centre is normally able to dictate the further course of events and exploit his command of space to gain even more ground. Thus, controlling the centre is not so much an end in itself as a step towards an overall control of the board, which in turn provides the right strategic conditions for the successful handling of the forces.

The Pawn Formation

Any reference to *the* pawn formation is usually understood to cover the placing of both White's and Black's pawns at a given point in the game. The two sets, provided that they are not entirely out of balance numerically, are interdependent and valued in terms of each other: the superiority of one player's is a measure of the inferiority of his opponent's.

The pawns have a lasting influence on the character of the position because they are so much slower and more restricted in their movements than the pieces are. Being unable to move horizontally or backwards, they can never return to a square once they have left it. Every step taken represents a definite change in the situation, for better or worse.

While there is no reason why pawns should not be employed tactically, their chief duty is to control squares and maintain a line of defence. At the beginning of the game the pawns are ideally stationed from a defensive point of view, as all the squares on the third rank are protected, most of them doubly. But if the pieces are to get into action, then at least one or two pawn moves are inevitable. The player's problem, therefore, is to find ways of advancing his pawns without leaving weak spots which the enemy can attack. Diagram 70 illustrates a typical formation where this is satisfactorily achieved.

70. Classical Pawn Formation This set-up enables all the pieces to get into active play and assures a lively clash in the centre. The presence there of two white pawns as against one black shows who has the initiative: White's QP is agressive; Black's defensive.

Black's two pawn moves have not created any weaknesses, for every square on the third rank still enjoys the protection of a pawn. White, on the other hand has advanced his QBP as well, thereby committing his Q3 to the charge of his pieces for the rest of the game. However, having the initiative, he need not think in terms of defence, and in any case, though his pawn line is more extended, it remains unbroken.

Pawn Chains

In the set-up shown in Diagram 70 a state of tension exists between White's QP and Black's KP: each can capture the other. In such circumstances both players must take care lest the opponent obtain an advantage by capturing, and for that reason the contending pawns are often supported by a colleague (in this instance White's QBP and Black's QP). But White also has another course of action: he can advance his QP to the fifth rank (i.e. alongside Black's KP) and by so doing free himself of the continual necessity to reckon up the advantages and disadvantages of the pawn captures. All the tension is immediately resolved and the four centre pawns are locked together, unable to move. This type of formation is known as a 'chain' formation and gives the play a clear strategic character, as illustrated in Diagram 71.

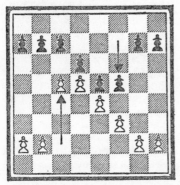

71. Chain-Formation Strategy

The general plan for both players is to attack on the side where they control more space. Thus, here White would normally advance on the Queen's wing, while Black would counter on the King's. The arrows indicate the two separate lines of assault.

The blocking of the pawns has the effect of stabilising the situation and of dividing the board diagonally in two —it is as if a wall is suddenly thrown up at an angle between the armies. With direct progress at a halt, the players turn their energies to undermining the opposing chain from the side, and this process is shown in full swing in the above diagram. The division of the territory, which is never exactly equal, decides who has the overall initiative. In this example it is White. But while he has more room than Black in which to manœuvre, his pawns are by the same token easier to attack; in addition, he has more squares behind his lines which could prove weak (i.e. his Q3, Q4 and K3 compared with Black's K3). All this leads to the conclusion that establishing a pawn chain extending to the fifth rank or beyond is an ambitious step and one which can only be justified if the pieces are in a position to occupy and exploit the ground gained.

It is possible for a single pawn to form the leading link of two pawn chains at once. The result is a 'wedge' formation, as shown in Diagram 72. As pawn wedges

72. Wedge-Formation Strategy

Here the general plan for both sides is to seek to undermine either the enemy QBP or KP by advancing the neighbouring QKtP or KBP, as indicated by the arrows. The choice and timing of these thrusts depends on the particular circumstances.

are mostly found either near or in the centre, their effect is usually to bring active operations to a stop in that area of the board and to divert the players' efforts to the wings. Other things being equal, the point of the wedge restricts the movements of the opponent's pieces and is therefore often the decisive factor in the struggle for the initiative.

But again, the weakening of squares behind the pawns is a potential hazard; for example, in the above formation White's Q4 would be an ideal post for an enemy Knight or Bishop.

Open Files

As soon as a pawn makes a capture in a game or is itself removed from the board a gap is created on the file on which it stood. This circumstance is very important, and every such opening in the pawn lines has a bearing on the general nature of the position. A typical case is illustrated in Diagram 73. Here the QB file for White and the K file for Black form obvious avenues of attack for the pieces.

73. Two Half-Open Files
This formation is normally the result of an exchange of pawns on Black's Q4: the capturing white QBP is recaptured by the KP. The two files have each been opened from one end but remain occupied by a pawn at the other.

The Rooks have most to gain from the opening of files, being ideally placed for aggression if in control of one which is open down its whole length. Diagram 74 is an example of such a situation.

It is no accident that one of the white Rooks is stationed at QB5, for this is an 'outpost' point, i.e. a square on an open file that is both in enemy territory and protected by a pawn. The Rook is secure there, as Black cannot drive it away by . . . , P-QKt3 without leaving a worse weakness at QB3.

74. Controlling an Open File
The white Rooks have an unchallenged hold on the QB file. Since it is the only open file and therefore the key area of conflict between the forces, White enjoys a clear strategic advantage. Black is entirely on the defensive.

The Seventh and Eighth Ranks
The domination of an open file is not an end in itself; it is the logical prelude to an invasion of the seventh and eighth ranks by the major pieces. A straightforward illustration is provided by Diagram 75.

75. Successful Invasion
The white Rook and Queen have penetrated as far as possible on the QB file and now turn to other conquests. Black's QKtP, Knight and Rook even face extinction, while his K side is also in danger. White wins easily.

The two back (first and second) ranks are the most vulnerable in a player's camp because none of the squares on them can be directly covered by his pawns. As the game progresses and more pawn and piece exchanges occur the risk of an enemy breakthrough increases, until by the time the endgame is reached invading pieces can often no longer be kept out even with correct defence. A Rook on the seventh rank plays havoc with defenceless pawns, while two Rooks so placed constitute one of the most prized objectives in chess. Thus, in Diagram 76 not only are

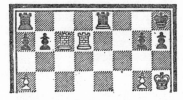

76. Seventh Rank Exploited
The commanding position of the white Rooks more than balances the material deficit. Black must fight, for a draw.

Black's Q-side pawns liable to fall but the safety of his King is also threatened.

Sometimes in positions where all seems lost, Rooks doubled on the seventh rank can save the game by giving perpetual check—indeed, they may go further and force mate. This could happen, for instance, in the above situation, given a slight alteration (Black's Rook on K1 to KB1 and his King to KKt1): if it is White's move, he wins by 1 RxP ch, K-R1; 2 RxP ch, K-Kt1; 3 R (B7)-Kt7 mate.

Pawn Weaknesses
Each line of pawns is perfect at the start of the game, but as changes take place in them they begin to lose their flexibility and become more likely to break up. Every time a file (R files excepted) is opened either a pawn or a group of pawns is isolated from the rest and thereby weakened—theoretically, at least. The extent to which these 'islands' of pawns may be a real handicap depends chiefly on how many there are. The fewer the better, in principle, but the best number in practice is generally two, with either four pawns in one and three in the other or five and two (if a player has only six pawns left, the soundest

69

groupings are three and three or four and two). A comparison of the advantages and disadvantages of some typical pawn configurations is provided by the four diagrams 77, 78, 79 and 80.

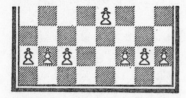

77. Aggressive Formation
The KP occupies and contests the centre; the open file gives the pieces freedom; there are no weaknesses.

78. Resilient Formation
The QP and KP defend the centre and can counter-attack by advancing, given the chance; QKt3 is a weak point.

79. Favourable for White
Here the superiority of two islands over three is clear: Black's pawns are scattered and lack co-ordination. White will attack down the centre files, use K5 as an outpost and force his opponent to guard the 'backward' KP with pieces.

These examples clearly show that in normal circumstances pawns are stronger united with others than separated. An isolated pawn is weak for two main reasons: first, it cannot be defended by another pawn and consequently, if attacked, requires a piece to guard it—which

80. Favourable for Black
A single, compact group of pawns is invariably stronger than three disjointed ones. There are no weaknesses in Black's formation, but White's embodies two pawns that are cut off from all colleagues. They will tie him to passive defence.

is uneconomical; second, the square in front of it, being without pawn protection, makes an ideal base for the enemy. As a rule, therefore, isolated pawns are avoided unless other factors are involved which offset the inherent disadvantages. The most important type of formation where this is the case is illustrated in Diagram 81.

81. The Isolated QP
Black has the sounder pawns and a strong operational point at Q4. However, the QP occupies the centre, provides outposts at QB5 and K5 and guarantees White more space in which to deploy his pieces for attacking purposes.

White must follow an aggressive plan, seeking to exploit his opening initiative and greater freedom of action. Black, on the other hand, aims to reduce the force of his opponent's threats by exchanging pieces or by keeping them tied to the defence of the QP. The chances are delicately balanced.

71

When a pawn makes a capture and moves on to a file that has a colleague on it the two are described as 'doubled' pawns. Pawns that have been doubled, like those shown in Diagram 82, are invariably weaker than they were

82. Doubled Pawns
This common formation is usually the result of an exchange of pieces on QB3: Black recaptured with his QP.

before. They have considerable defensive strength in conjunction with the next pawn, but their capacity for active play is extremely limited. The front one blocks the path of the other, thus making them little more effective than a single pawn.

Pawns that are both doubled and isolated, as illustrated in Diagram 83, can become a terrible liability. Not only

83. Doubled, Isolated Pawns
Capturing on KB3 has wrecked the pawn line on the K side, which is now riddled with weaknesses.

do they have the limitations mentioned above but they also need pieces to protect them. The result is often the paralysis of an entire wing.

It occasionally happens that three pawns find themselves 'tripled' on a file. As they are usually isolated as well, it stands to reason that on average they only have a small part of their original value. Their long-term prospects are especially bad, for they offer a ready target in the endgame, where even minor faults in the pawn formation may be hard to conceal.

72

Strong Pawns

A pawn is normally described as 'sound' if it is not weak in any respect. The word 'strong' implies more: that the pawn is a positive strategic advantage; in other words, it is not just a neutral factor but the direct opposite of a weakness.

Whereas weak pawns are either passive or a responsibility to the pieces, aggressiveness is the essential quality of strong pawns. In the majority of instances, therefore, they are located in the opponent's half of the board. Diagram 84 shows an ideal case, the consequence of some very

84. Dominant Pawns
The white QP and KP have secured a stranglehold on the position, occupying the centre unopposed and leaving Black with scarcely any room for his pieces beyond the second rank. He is doomed to a campaign of passive defence.

poor play by Black. It illustrates strikingly the role of the pawns in controlling space and making it safe for the pieces. White has a free hand in the centre and can mass his forces there for action wherever they are required.

As a pawn advances into enemy territory its chances of eventually gaining promotion improve, particularly if it is strongly backed up. Many difficulties lie ahead, however, and its prospects of reaching the eighth rank do not become real until the resistance of the opposing pawns can be overcome. A pawn which has successfully achieved this is thereafter known as a 'passed' pawn, for that, as Diagram 85 shows, is exactly what it has done.

85. A Passed Pawn
The white QP can no longer be challenged by a pawn: there is no enemy QP present to bar the way, while it has passed out of the range of the black QBP and KP. Its advance · will have to be checked by pieces.

A passed pawn's strength depends greatly on how far it has progressed and how well it is supported. Obviously, a pawn on the verge of being promoted is an immediate and serious threat to the defence. However, one which is not so far forward but more securely protected, like that in Diagram 86, for example, may prove still more damaging in the long run; for while the pieces that would other-

86. A Protected Passed Pawn
Pawns like the QBP here are supremely strong because they are almost immune to attack. They first have to be undermined.

wise have given it their backing are free to turn their attention elsewhere, those on the defending side must always be prepared to deal with its advance, and that very often leads to their being overburdened with tasks. A protected passed pawn thus gives the chess axiom that 'the threat is stronger than the execution' real meaning and form. With one a player can put pressure on his opponent without committing himself unduly—which is the ideal position to be in, strategically speaking.

74

King Location

Owing to their unique status the Kings are always either directly or indirectly involved in matters of strategy. Safety is the important factor, and that naturally depends on the material on the board and its deployment in relation to the Kings.

When the pieces left are few in number and not strong enough to create sudden, overwhelming threats it is safe for the King to participate actively in events. Its ability to cover all adjoining squares gives it an advantage at close quarters over every piece except the Queen; not even the powerful Rook is its equal at in-fighting. In the endgame, therefore, the King has a special strategic role: to combat the enemy King in a struggle for territory. The side whose King gets the upper hand in this duel and forces its way into the opposing camp first normally wins, while just a slight spacial advantage, such as is illustrated in Diagram 87, may be sufficient to settle the issue.

87. Duelling Kings
The white King has won the struggle for control of the centre. It can exploit this by advancing to QB5: then the threat of either penetrating to QKt6 or swinging back via the fifth rank to attack the KKtP is decisive.

In the earlier stages of the game it is rarely possible for the King to do anything except shelter behind the pawns on one of the wings. If it remains at K1 for long, it runs the risk of being attacked—this is especially true when a central file can be opened—and of losing the right to castle. Should that happen, the King becomes a strategic liability, as is clear from Diagram 88.

88. White in Difficulties
Being no longer able to castle, White needs many moves to sort out his K-side pieces. In that time Black can castle, occupy the open K file with a Rook and launch a powerful attack. White's extra pawn is quite worthless.

How secure the King is after it has castled is chiefly determined by the soundness of its pawn cover. In general, the more the pawns in front of the King have been moved the less they are able to ward off attackers. Thus, in Diagram 89 Black is powerless to resist the enemy Queen's

89. A Loosened King Position
Black's K side is full of weaknesses: the pawns no longer defend the third rank and the white squares KB4 and KR4 are similarly vulnerable.

threats. It can give perpetual check by itself on KKt6 and KR6, while with the support of another piece (such as a Knight at KR5 or a Bishop on the QKt1-KR7 diagonal) it would force mate next move. This example shows how closely connected are the three principal strategic elements. At KKt6 the white Queen commands part of the board that has been surrendered by the opposing pawns and which is important because of the presence nearby of the black King.

When the Kings are both safely entrenched behind the pawn lines and in no danger of being seriously threatened for some time their involvement in the struggle is indirect or negative. In such cases a player dare not commit himself to an attempt to decide the game by a mating attack for fear of its being repulsed with losses. The contest therefore takes a quieter course, with the two armies concentrating on other strategic targets. In Diagram 90,

90. Sound King Positions
White's pawns in front of the King are in perfect order. Black has made one slight concession in that he has moved his KRP, but as his King is also well protected by pieces, no trouble should arise on that account.

for instance, the Q side will be the main battlefield, and conquests made there (e.g. on the QB file) will probably amount to a winning advantage. Though the interplay of King location, the pawn formation and space control is not as obvious as in the previous example, nevertheless here too it is the key to the correct strategy.

Bishops of Opposite Colours

Owing to their dynamic qualities pieces are more concerned with carrying out strategic ideas than shaping them. However, the fact that individual Bishops are restricted to half the board can have odd effects when exchanges result in 'Bishops of opposite colours' (one player's operates on white squares and the other's on black). The impossibility of their ever coming to grips with each

other causes special problems, as is evident from Diagram
91. The essential point to note is that material often has
a purely nominal value.

91. A Clear Draw
Despite his material and
spacial superiority White can
achieve nothing. His op-
ponent's hold on the white
squares is permanent.

If the Bishops are a strong drawing factor in basic
endings, the reverse tends to be true when major pieces
are also present. Diagram 92 shows how useful the Bishop

92. White Wins
The extra pawns hinder Black
and his Bishop cannot counter
the enemy threats. He is
virtually a piece down.

may then prove in the execution of an attack. After
1 R-Kt7 ch, K-B1; 2 K-B6, R-Q1; 3 B-Q6 ch, K-K1; 4
KxP, RxB ch; 5 PxR White queens his pawn.

In positions with Bishops of opposite colours space, seen
chiefly in terms of diagonals, has a heightened role to play.
That apart, the principles of strategy are applied in the
usual way.

5

BASIC OPENING THEORY

The opening phase of the game, during which the mobilisation of the two armies takes place, has been a source of fascination since earliest times. The choice facing the players is immense. There are, for instance, 400 legal ways (the product of each side's 20 initial possibilities) of making the first move for White and Black, and with every new move the number is multiplied again. Out of this chaos there has gradually evolved a network of systems which, though differing in character, are all founded to a greater or lesser degree on the strategic concepts of control of space, sound pawns and King safety.

In the modern era the intensity of analytical research and practical play has caused such an expansion of theoretical knowledge that it is now commonplace for books to be entirely devoted to a single system—and even that is not enough. In one brief chapter, therefore, it is only possible to give a bare outline of a number of selected 'openings' and to indicate to what extent the respective objectives are fulfilled.

The overriding feature of the opening struggle is the fact that White has the initiative. He is able to deploy his men aggressively and pursue a course of positive action. Black, on the other hand, being a 'tempo' behind, must tread very carefully and not undertake more than is warranted. If he can counter White's threats and establish equality, he should not be dissatisfied.

Centre Game. 1 P-K4, P-K4; 2 P-Q4, PxP; 3 QxP. White makes an elemental assault on the centre with his pawns. The drawback is that 'developing' his Queen so early on an open board results in a loss of time. 3 . . . , Kt-QB3; 4 Q-K3, Kt-B3; 5 Kt-QB3, B-Kt5; 6 B-Q2, O-O; 7 O-O-O, R-K1. Black's prospects are good, for the white Queen remains awkwardly placed.

King's Gambit Accepted. 1 P-K4, P-K4; 2 P-KB4, PxP. White tackles the enemy KP from the other side, aiming for a central preponderance and a possible attack down the KB file. 3 Kt-KB3, P-Q4; 4 PxP, Kt-KB3; 5 P-B4, P-B3; 6 P-Q4, B-Kt5 ch; 7 Kt-B3, PxP; 8 BxP, O-O; 9 B-Q3, R-K1 ch; 10 B-K5, Kt-B3; 11 O-O. The game is approximately level.

93. Modern King's Gambit
The King's Gambit scored many successes in its heyday last century because Black often spoilt his King position trying to hold the gambit pawn by . . . , P-KKt4. The modern method of vigorous retaliation in the centre based on . . . , P-Q4 yields good counterplay.

Vienna Game. 1 P-K4, P-K4; 2 Kt-QB3. The intention is to play a delayed type of King's Gambit. 2 . . . , Kt-KB3; 3 P-B4, P-Q4; 4 BPxP, KtxP; 5 Kt-B3, B-K2; 6 P-Q4, O-O; 7 B-Q3, P-KB4; 8 PxP e.p., BxP; 9 O-O, Kt-B3. Energetic counterplay based on . . . , P-Q4 has again enabled Black to equalise.

Philidor Defence. 1 P-K4, P-K4; 2 Kt-KB3, P-Q3. Black

defends his attacked KP but at the cost of shutting in his King's Bishop. 3 P-Q4, Kt-KB3; 4 Kt-B3, QKt-Q2; 5 B-QB4, B-K2; 6 O-O, P-B3; 7 P-QR4, O-O; 8 Q-K2, P-KR3; 9 B-Kt3, Q-B2; 10 P-R3. Solid and rather passive describes Black's position.

Petroff Defence. 1 P-K4, P-K4; 2 Kt-KB3, Kt-KB3. Black aims for equality by means of counter-threats and rapid development. 3 P-Q4, KtxP; 4 B-Q3, P-Q4; 5 KtxP, B-Q3; 6 O-O, O-O; 7 P-QB4. As is usually the case in symmetrical positions, the first player preserves some initiative.

Scotch Game. 1 P-K4. P-K4; 2 Kt-KB3, Kt-QB3; 3 P-Q4. Having had his first threat parried by a sound developing move, White again tries to force matters in the centre. 3 . . . , PxP; 4 KtxP, Kt-B3; 5 Kt-QB3, B-Kt5; 6 KtxKt, KtPxKt; 7 B-Q3, P-Q4; 8 PxP, PxP; 9 O-O, O-O. Black has adequate counterplay.

Giuoco Piano. 1 P-K4, P-K4; 2 Kt-KB3, Kt-QB3; 3 B-B4, B-B4. There is now a choice between two distinct strategic plans.

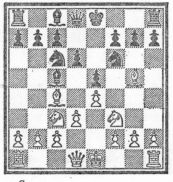

94. Classical Development
In this variation, often referred to as the **Giuoco Pianissimo** (Italian for 'Very Quiet Game'), both sides follow the simplest principles of development. No unnecessary pawn moves occur, while the minor pieces quickly post themselves near the centre.

(i) 4 P-Q3, Kt-B3; 5 Kt-B3, P-Q3; 6 B-KKt5. White has no more than a very slight initiative.

(ii) 4 P-B3, Kt-B3; 5 P-Q4, PxP; 6 PxP, B-Kt5 ch; 7 Kt-B3, KtxKP; 8 O-O, BxKt; 9 P-Q5—Möller Attack, the battle for the centre at its fiercest. 9 . . . , B-B3; 10 R-K1, Kt-K2; 11 RxKt, P-Q3; 12 B-Kt5, BxB; 13 KtxB. White's attacking chances balance the pawn sacrificed.

Evans Gambit. 1 P-K4, P-K4; 2 Kt-KB3, Kt-QB3; 3 B-B4, B-B4; 4 P-QKt4. White offers a pawn to gain time to build up a powerful centre. 4 . . . , BxP; 5 P-B3, B-R4; 6 P-Q4, P-Q3; 7 Q-Kt3, Q-Q2; 8 PxP, PxP; 9 B-R3, B-Kt3; 10 O-O, Kt-R4; 11 KtxP, KtxQ; 12 PxKt, Q-K3; 13 BxQ, BxB. By judiciously returning his extra material Black has neutralised all White's threats.

Two Knights' Defence. 1 P-K4, P-K4; 2 Kt-KB3, Kt-QB3; 3 B-B4, Kt-B3. Here Black stakes a pawn for freedom of action. 4 Kt-Kt5, P-Q4; 5 PxP, Kt-QR4; 6 B-Kt5 ch, P-B3; 7 PxP, PxP; 8 B-K2, P-KR3; 9 Kt-KB3, P-K5; 10 Kt-K5, B-Q3; 11 P-KB4, PxP e.p.; 12 KtxP(KB6), Q-B2; 13 O-O, O-O. Black has good play for a pawn.

Four Knights' Game. 1 P-K4, P-K4; 2 Kt-KB3, Kt-QB3; 3 Kt-B3, Kt-B3. Sound development on both sides is the feature here. 4 B-Kt5, B-Kt5; 5 O-O, O-O; 6 P-Q3, P-Q3; 7 B-Kt5, BxKt; 8 PxB, Q-K2; 9 R-K1, Kt-Q1; 10 P-Q4, Kt-K3. White's rather more aggressive position is offset by the doubled pawns.

Ruy Lopez. 1 P-K4, P-K4; 2 Kt-KB3, Kt-QB3; 3 B-Kt5. This is one of the strongest and most frequently played of all the openings. White employs refined methods of building up his position and makes it very difficult for the second player to equalise, despite the variety of defences at his disposal. These fall roughly into 'ancient' and 'modern' categories.

(i) 3 . . . , P-Q3—the Steinitz Defence, in which Black relies on simple development. 4 P-Q4, B-Q2; 5 Kt-B3, Kt-B3; 6 O-O, B-K2; 7 R-K1, PxP; 8 KtxP, O-O (see Diagram 95); 9 BxKt, PxB; 10 B-Kt5, R-K1; 11 Q-Q3,

95. Solid Defence
While Black has avoided creating weaknesses in his camp, he has been obliged to give ground in the centre by exchanging pawns. Because of their general rigidity the Steinitz and most of the other old defences are rarely encountered now.

P-KR3; 12 B-R4, Kt-R2; 13 BxB, RxB. White has the more active position.

(ii) 3 . . . ; Kt-B3—the Berlin Defence, an immediate counter-attack on the white KP. 4 O-O, KtxP; 5 P-Q4, B-K2; 6 Q-K2, Kt-Q3; 7 BxKt, KtPxB; 8 PxP, Kt-Kt2; 9 Kt-B3, O-O; 10 Kt-Q4. Black is cramped and awkwardly placed on the Q side.

(iii) 3 . . . , B-B4—the Classical Defence, in which Black seeks better prospects for his King's Bishop than it usually obtains from K2. 4 P-B3, Kt-B3; 5 O-O, O-O; 6 P-Q4, B-Kt3; 7 R-K1, P-Q3; 8 P-KR3. White retains the initiative.

(iv) 3 . . . , P-B4—the Schliemann Defence, a sharp and risky attempt to secure quick counterplay. 4 Kt-B3, PxP; 5 QKtxP, P-Q4; 6 KtxP, PxKt; 7 KtxKt, Q-Q4; 8 P-QB4, Q-Q3; 9 KtxP ch, B-Q2; 10 BxB ch, QxB; 11 Kt-Kt5, Kt-B3; 12 O-O, B-B4; 13 P-Q4, PxP e.p.;

14 R-K1 ch, K-B2; 15 B-K3. It is doubtful whether the passed QP affords Black sufficient compensation for the pawn sacrificed.

(v) **3 . . . , P-QR3; 4 BxKt**—the **Exchange Variation,** by which White aims to exploit the doubling of the enemy QBPs. **4 . . . , QPxB; 5 Kt-B3, P-B3; 6 P-Q4, PxP; 7 QxP, QxQ; 8 KtxQ, B-Q3; 9 B-K3, Kt-K2; 10 O-O-O, B-Q2; 11 Kt-Kt3, O-O-O.** The Bishop pair ensures Black good play. The advance of the QRP on the third move, which this variation puts to the test, is the key to the modern defensive systems.

(vi) **3 . . . , P-QR3; 4 B-R4, P-Q3**—the **Steinitz Defence Deferred,** an improved version of the old defence. **5 P-B3, B-Q2; 6 P-Q4, Kt-B3; 7 O-O, B-K2; 8 R-K1, O-O; 9 QKt-Q2, R-K1.** Though somewhat cramped, Black maintains a firm hold on the centre.

(vii) **3 . . . , P-QR3; 4 B-R4, Kt-B3; 5 O-O, KtxP**—the **Open Defence,** a bid for free play by Black. **6 P-Q4, P-QKt4; 7 B-Kt3, P-Q4; 8 PxP, B-K3; 9 P-B3, B-K2; 10 QKt-Q2, O-O; 11 Q-K2, Kt-B4; 12 Kt-Q4, KtxB; 13 QKtxKt, Q-Q2; 14 KtxKt, QxKt; 15 B-K3.** White has some attacking prospects based on the advance of his KBP.

(viii) **3 . . . , P-QR3; 4 B-R4, Kt-B3; 5 O-O, B-K2; 6 R-K1, P-QKt4; 7 B-Kt3, O-O; 8 P-B3, P-Q4**—the **Marshall Attack,** a daring pawn sacrifice for the initiative. **9 PxP, KtxP; 10 KtxP, KtxKt; 11 RxKt, P-QB3; 12 P-Q4, B-Q3; 13 R-K1, Q-R5; 14 P-Kt3, Q-R6; 15 B-K3, B-KKt5; 16 Q-Q3, QR-K1; 17 Kt-Q2, R-K3.** Black's threats may just balance the lost material.

(ix) **3 . . . , P-QR3; 4 B-R4, Kt-B3; 5 O-O, B-K2; 6 R-K1, P-QKt4; 7 B-Kt3, P-Q3; 8 P-B3, O-O; 9 P-KR3, Kt-Kt1**—the **Breyer Variation,** in which Black regroups his Queen's Knight at Q2. **10 P-Q4, QKt-Q2; 11 QKt-Q2, B-Kt2; 12 B-B2, R-K1; 13 Kt-B1, B-KB1; 14 Kt-Kt3,**

P-Kt3. Both sides have fulfilled their opening tasks satisfactorily.

96. Flexible Defence
Black has held his ground in the centre and prepared himself for action on any part of the board White may select. This variation typifies the greater flexibility of the modern defences and is currently Black's most popular choice.

(x) 3 . . . , P-QR3; 4 B-R4, Kt-B3; 5 O-O, B-K2; 6 R-K1, P-QKt4; 7 B-Kt3, P-Q3; 8 P-B3, O-O; 9 P-KR3, Kt-QR4; 10 B-B2, P-B4; 11 P-Q4, Q-B2—the Tchigorin Defence, Black's most orthodox response. 12 QKt-Q2, B-Q2; 13 Kt-B1, BPxP; 14 PxP, QR-B1; 15 R-K2, KR-K1; 16 Kt-Kt3, P-Kt3; 17 B-Kt5. White exerts some pressure in the centre and on the K side.

Centre Counter Defence. 1 P-K4, P-Q4. Challenging the enemy KP at once is considered premature, for it involves a loss of time. 2 PxP, Kt-KB3; 3 P-Q4, KtxP; 4 P-QB4, Kt-Kt3; 5 Kt-KB3, P-Kt3; 6 Kt-B3, B-Kt2; 7 P-KR3, O-O; 8 B-K3, Kt-B3; 9 Q-Q2. White's spacial advantage assures him good prospects.

French Defence. 1 P-K4, P-K3. Here Black first prepares the advance of his QP. The tempo of the struggle is slower and strategic themes come to the fore.

(i) 2 P-Q4, P-Q4; 3 P-K5—the **Advance Variation,** whereby White aims to establish a lasting spacial superiority on the K side. 3 . . . , P-QB4; 4 P-QB3,

Kt-QB3; 5 Kt-B3, Q-Kt3; 6 B-K2, PxP; 7 PxP, Kt-R3;
8 P-QKt3, Kt-B4; 9 B-Kt2, B-Kt5 ch; 10 K-B1, P-KR4.
Black's counterplay is adequate.

(ii) 2 P-Q4, P-Q4; 3 Kt-QB3, PxP—the Rubinstein
Variation, which is designed to ease Black's problems by
promoting exchanges. 4 KtxP, Kt-Q2; 5 Kt-KB3, KKt-B3;
6 KtxKt ch, KtxKt; 7 B-Q3, P-B4; 8 PxP, Q-R4 ch;
9 P-B3, QxBP; 10 B-Kt5, B-K2; 11 Q-K2, B-Q2; 12 Kt-K5.
White is aggressively placed.

(iii) 2 P-Q4, P-Q4; 3 Kt-QB3, B-Kt5—the Winawer
Variation, where Black is seen at his most challenging.
4 P-K5, P-QB4; 5 P-QR3, BxKt ch; 6 PxB, Kt-K2;
7 Q-Kt4, PxP; 8 QxKtP, R-Kt1; 9 QxP, Q-B2; 10 Kt-K2,
QKt-B3; 11 P-KB4, B-Q2; 12 R-QKt1, O-O-O; 13 Q-Q3,
PxP. The complications offer chances to both sides.

(iv) 2 P-Q4, P-Q4; 3 Kt-QB3, Kt-KB3; 4 B-Kt5, B-K2;
5 P-K5, KKt-Q2; 6 BxB, QxB—the Classical Variation,
the most logical expression of White's strategy. 7 P-B4,
O-O; 8 Kt-B3, P-QB4; 9 B-Q3, P-B3 (see Diagram 97);

97. Centre Pawns in Conflict
Black strives to destroy the
enemy pawn centre, which at
present cramps his whole
game. As White cannot successfully maintain his QP and
KP, he exchanges them off
and plays for control of the
squares that they vacate.

10 QPxP, Kt-B3; 11 PxP, QxKBP; 12 P-KKt3, KtxP;
13 O-O, B-Q2; 14 Q-Q2, B-K1; 15 QR-K1. Black feels
the absence of his King's Bishop, which could have covered
the weak points at Q3 and K4.

(v) 2 P-Q4, P-Q4; 3 Kt-Q2—the Tarrasch Variation, by which White retains his central options and avoids the pin by . . . ., B-Kt5. 3 . . . , P-QB4; 4 KPxP, KPxP; 5 B-Kt5 ch, Kt-B3; 6 KKt-B3, B-Q3; 7 O-O, Kt-K2; 8 PxP, BxP; 9 Kt-Kt3, B-Kt3; 10 B-K3, BxB; 11 BxKt ch, PxB; 12 PxB, O-O; 13 Q-Q2, Q-Kt3; 14 Q-B3, P-QR4. Black has practically equalised.

Caro-Kann Defence. 1 P-K4, P-QB3. This allows Black to challenge the white KP without blocking the path of his Queen's Bishop.

(i) 2 Kt-QB3, P-Q4; 3 Kt-B3—the Two Knights' Variation, in which White avoids showing his hand at first. 3 . . . , B-Kt5; 4 P-KR3, BxKt; 5 QxB, Kt-B3; 6 P-Q3, P-K3; 7 P-QR3, QKt-Q2; 8 P-KKt3, P-KKt3; 9 B-Kt2, B-Kt2; 10 O-O, O-O; 11 Q-K2, Kt-K1; 12 K-R2, P-KB4. Black has a very solid position.

(ii) 2 P-Q4, P-Q4; 3 PxP, PxP; 4 P-QB4—the Panov Attack, which immediately brings about a very delicate struggle. 4 . . . , Kt-KB3; 5 Kt-QB3, P-K3; 6 Kt-B3, B-K2; 7 P-B5, O-O; 8 B-Q3, P-QKt3; 9 P-QKt4, P-QR4; 10 Kt-QR4, QKt-Q2; 11 P-QR3, RPxP; 12 RPxP, PxP; 13 KtPxP, P-K4. White's action on the wing has been countered correctly.

(iii) 2 P-Q4, P-Q4; 3 Kt-QB3, PxP; 4 KtxP, Kt-Q2—the Smyslov Variation, in which Black relies on slow but sure development. 5 B-QB4, KKt-B3; 6 Kt-Kt5, P-K3; 7 Q-K2, Kt-Kt3; 8 B-Q3, P-KR3; 9 QKt-B3, P-B4; 10 PxP, BxP; 11 Kt-K5, QKt-Q4; 12 P-QR3, B-Q3; 13 KKt-B3, Q-B2; 14 O-O, O-O; 15 P-B4, Kt-K2. White's initiative is insignificant.

(iv) 2 P-Q4, P-Q4; 3 Kt-QB3, PxP; 4 KtxP, B-B4—the Classical Variation, Black's simplest and most natural system. 5 Kt-Kt3, B-Kt3; 6 P-KR4, P-KR3; 7 Kt-B3, Kt-Q2; 8 B-Q3, BxB; 9 QxB, Q-B2; 10 B-Q2,

KKt-B3; 11 O-O-O, P-K3; 12 K-Kt1, O-O-O; 13 P-B4, P-B4; 14 B-B3, PxP; 15 KtxP, P-R3. White has a minimal advantage.

Sicilian Defence. 1 P-K4, P-QB4. In essence a counter-attack, this defence is a very popular weapon. It is rich in variations and offers good chances on the Queen's wing. But White often obtains lasting pressure on the K side.

(i) 2 P-Q4, PxP; 3 P-QB3—the Morra Gambit, a bid to open up the game as rapidly as possible. 3 . . . , Kt-KB3; 4 P-K5, Kt-Q4; 5 B-QB4, Q-B2; 6 Q-K2, Kt-Kt3; 7 B-Q3, Kt-B3; 8 Kt-B3, P-Q4; 9 P-KR3, PxP; 10 KtxP. The delayed acceptance of the pawn has crossed White's plans.

(ii) 2 Kt-KB3, Kt-QB3; 3 P-Q4, PxP; 4 KtxP, Kt-B3; 5 Kt-QB3, P-K3—the Four Knights' Variation, a very old line based on straightforward development. 6 KKt-Kt5, B-Kt5; 7 P-QR3, BxKt ch; 8 KtxB, P-Q4; 9 PxP, PxP; 10 B-Q3, O-O; 11 O-O, P-KR3; 12 B-KB4. White has the sounder position.

(iii) 2 Kt-KB3, Kt-QB3; 3 P-Q4, PxP; 4 KtxP, Kt-B3; 5 Kt-QB3, P-Q3; 6 B-KKt5—the Rauzer Variation, one of White's strongest attacking systems. 6 . . . , P-K3; 7 Q-Q2, B-K2; 8 O-O-O, O-O; 9 P-B4, KtxKt; 10 QxKt, P-KR3; 11 B-R4, Q-R4; 12 B-B4. Black is under pressure in the centre and on the K side.

(iv) 2 Kt-KB3, Kt-QB3; 3 P-Q4, PxP; 4 KtxP, Kt-B3; 5 Kt-QB3, P-Q3; 6 B-K2, P-K4—the Boleslavsky Variation, in which Black risks a backward QP for the sake of freer development for his pieces. 7 Kt-Kt3, B-K2; 8 O-O, O-O; 9 B-K3, B-K3; 10 B-B3, Kt-QR4; 11 KtxKt, QxKt. Black enjoys sufficient counterplay.

(v) 2 Kt-KB3, P-Q3; 3 P-Q4, PxP; 4 KtxP, Kt-KB3; 5 Kt-QB3, P-KKt3—the Dragon Variation, where Black's object is to combine action on the QB file and the long black diagonal. 6 B-K2, B-Kt2; 7 B-K3, Kt-B3; 8 O-O, O-O; 9 Kt-Kt3, B-K3; 10 P-B4, Q-B1; 11 P-KR3, R-Q1; 12 Kt-Q4, KtxKt; 13 BxKt, B-B5. The game is about even.

(vi) 2 Kt-KB3, P-Q3; 3 P-Q4, PxP; 4 KtxP, Kt-KB3; 5 Kt-QB3, P-KKt3; 6 B-K3, B-Kt2; 7 P-B3, O-O; 8 Q-Q2 —the Anti-Dragon Attack, which threatens to put Black's defences to a severe test. 8 . . . , Kt-B3; 9 O-O-O (see Diagram 98), KtxKt; 10 BxKt, B-K3; 11 K-Kt1, Q-B2;

98. The 'Dragon' in Danger
This aggressive system, a typical product of the modern approach, has deprived the 'fianchettoed' (i.e. developed on Kt2) Bishop of much of its bite. Unless Black takes immediate, energetic steps to obtain counterplay, he will be overrun on the KR file.

12 P-KR4, KR-B1; 13 P-R5, Q-R4; 14 PxP, RPxP; 15 P-R3, QR-Kt1. The game is finely balanced.

(vii) 2 Kt-KB3, P-Q3; 3 P-Q4, PxP; 4 KtxP, Kt-KB3; 5 Kt-QB3, P-QR3—the Najdorf Variation, which has the merit of great flexibility. 6 B-Kt5, P-K3; 7 P-B4, B-K2; 8 Q-B3, Q-B2; 9 O-O-O, QKt-Q2; 10 P-KKt4, P-Kt4; 11 BxKt, KtxB; 12 P-Kt5, Kt-Q2; 13 P-QR3, R-QKt1. A fierce struggle is developing across the entire front.

(viii) 2 Kt-KB3, P-K3; 3 P-Q4, PxP; 4 KtxP, P-QR3; —the Kan Variation, in which Black tries to expand at once on the Q side. 5 Kt-QB3, Q-B2; 6 B-Q3, P-QKt4; 7 O-O, B-Kt2; 8 R-K1, B-B4; 9 B-K3, Q-Kt3; 10 Kt-Kt3, BxB; 11 RxB. White has a strong initiative.

(ix) 2 Kt-KB3, P-K3; 3 P-Q4, PxP; 4 KtxP, Kt-QB3— the Taimanov Variation, the latest trend in Black's search for a diversion on the flank. 5 Kt-Kt5, P-Q3; 6 B-KB4, P-K4; 7 B-K3, Kt-B3; 8 QKt-B3, P-QR3; 9 Kt-R3, P-QKt4; 10 Kt-Q5, R-QKt1. White's formation is intrinsically superior.

(x) 2 Kt-KB3, P-K3; 3 P-Q4, PxP; 4 KtxP, Kt-KB3; 5 Kt-QB3, P-Q3; 6 B-K2, P-QR3; 7 O-O, QKt-Q2—the Paulsen Variation, by which Black aims for resilience in the centre in conjunction with activity on the Queen's wing. 8 P-B4, P-QKt4; 9 B-B3, B-Kt2; 10 P-QR3, Q-B2; 11 Q-K1, B-K2; 12 K-R1, R-QKt1; 13 P-QKt3, O-O; 14 B-Kt2, KR-K1. The game is evenly balanced.

(xi) 2 Kt-KB3, P-K3; 3 P-Q4, PxP; 4 KtxP, Kt-KB3; 5 Kt-QB3, P-Q3; 6 B-K2, P-QR3; 7 O-O, Kt-B3—the Scheveningen Variation, a firm but defensive system. 8 B-K3, B-K2; 9 P-B4, Q-B2; 10 Q-K1, O-O; 11 R-Q1. White has attacking chances on the K side.

(xii) 2 Kt-QB3, Kt-QB3; 3 P-KKt3, P-KKt3; 4 B-Kt2, B-Kt2; 5 P-Q3—the Closed Variation, in which White plans a slow advance on the King's wing and avoids a sharp clash in the centre. 5 . . . , P-Q3; 6 KKt-K2, P-K3; 7 B-K3, Kt-Q5; 8 Q-Q2, Q-R4; 9 O-O, Kt-K2; 10 K-R1, B-Q2; 11 P-B4, R-QKt1. Black has preserved a flexible position and is ready to counter-attack.

Alekhine Defence. 1 P-K4, Kt-KB3. The point of developing the Knight immediately is to provoke White into establishing a pawn centre that will prove difficult to maintain.

(i) 2 P-K5, Kt-Q4; 3 P-QB4, Kt-Kt3; 4 P-Q4, P-Q3; 5 P-B4—the Four Pawns' Attack, in which White accepts the challenge to the full. 5 . . . , PxP; 6 BPxP, Kt-B3; 7 B-K3, B-B4; 8 Kt-QB3, P-K3; 9 B-K2, B-K2; 10 Kt-B3, O-O; 11 O-O, P-B3; 12 PxP, BxP. Pressure on the QP almost compensates for the isolated KP.

(ii) 2 P-K5, Kt-Q4; 3 P-Q4, P-Q3; 4 Kt-KB3—the

Modern Variation, which reserves the option of advancing the QBP until the most favourable moment. **4 . . . , B-Kt5; 5 B-K2, P-K3; 6 O-O, B-K2; 7 P-KR3, B-R4; 8 P-B4, Kt-Kt3; 9 PxP, PxP; 10 Kt-B3, Kt-B3; 11 P-QKt3, O-O; 12 B-K3.** The initiative remains with White.

Robatsch Defence. 1 P-K4, P-KKt3; 2 P-Q4, B-Kt2. Black commits himself as little as possible, trusting that the basic soundness of his position will enable him to beat off White's threats. **3 Kt-KB3, P-Q3; 4 Kt-B3, Kt-Q2; 5 B-QB4, Kt-Kt3; 6 B-Kt3, P-QB3; 7 P-QR4, P-QR4; 8 O-O, P-K3; 9 B-K3, Kt-K2.** White has obtained some advantage in space, but the real clash is yet to come.

99. Ultramodern Defence
This position presents a striking contrast between direct, classical development and the more subtle kind. Flexible formations like Black's are a recent phenomenon. Once considered quite incorrect, they are gradually taking their place among the regular systems.

Blackmar Gambit. 1 P-Q4, P-Q4; 2 P-K4. The fundamental difference between the King's Pawn and the Queen's Pawn openings is that in the latter it is more difficult to advance the other centre pawn to the fourth rank: the K4 square is unprotected. When attempted on the 2nd move it involves a pawn sacrifice. **2 . . . , PxP; 3 Kt-QB3, Kt-KB3; 4 P-B3, PxP; 5 KtxP, P-KKt3; 6 B-QB4, B-Kt2; 7 Kt-K5, O-O; 8 B-KKt5, QKt-Q2; 9 O-O, P-B3.** White's initiative is not enough compensation for the pawn.

91

Queen's Gambit Accepted. 1 P-Q4, P-Q4; 2 P-QB4, PxP. The idea behind advancing the QBP is to try to clear the way for P-K4. In accepting the challenge, Black relies on soon being able to hit back in the centre himself.

(i) 3 Kt-KB3, Kt-KB3; 4 P-K3, P-K3; 5 BxP, P-B4; 6 O-O, P-QR3; 7 P-QR4—the Classical Variation, which prevents Black's intended expansion on the Queen's wing. 7 . . . , Kt-B3; 8 Q-K2, PxP; 9 R-Q1, B-K2; 10 PxP, O-O; 11 Kt-B3. Black has the sounder position but is under some pressure.

(ii) 3 Kt-KB3, Kt-KB3; 4 P-K3, P-K3; 5 BxP, P-B4; 6 O-O, P-QR3; 7 Q-K2, P-QKt4—the Modern Variation, in which both sides carry their strategies to a logical conclusion. 8 B-Kt3, B-Kt2; 9 R-Q1, QKt-Q2; 10 Kt-B3, Q-Kt1; 11 P-Q5, KtxP; 12 KtxKt, BxKt; 13 BxB, PxB; 14 RxP, B-K2; 15 P-K4, Q-Kt2. The game is level.

Queen's Gambit Declined. After 1 P-Q4, P-Q4; 2 P-QB4 Black has a wide selection of other defences at his disposal.

(i) **Slav Defence.** 2 . . . , P-QB3. Black gives his QP solid support. 3 Kt-KB3, Kt-B3; 4 Kt-B3, PxP; 5 P-QR4, B-B4; 6 P-K3, P-K3; 7 BxP, B-QKt5; 8 O-O, O-O (see Diagram 100); 9 Q-K2, QKt-Q2; 10 P-K4,

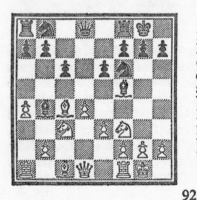

100. Quiet Defence
Black has solved most of his development problems but contented himself with a conservative, sound pawn set-up. White's QP stands unchallenged at present, and he can play to increase his hold on the centre by carrying through the advance of his KP.

B-Kt3; 11 B-Q3, P-KR3; 12 B-KB4, Q-K2. Black must be prepared for a lengthy defensive campaign.

(ii) **Semi-Slav Defence.** 2 . . . , P-QB3; 3 Kt-KB3, Kt-B3; 4 Kt-B3, P-K3. Here Black strengthens his QP still further prior to embarking on freeing operations on the Q side. 5 P-K3, QKt-Q2; 6 B-Q3, PxP; 7 BxBP, P-QKt4; 8 B-Q3, P-QR3; 9 P-K4, P-B4; 10 P-K5, PxP. The complications offer both players chances.

(iii) **Orthodox Defence.** 2 . . . , P-K3; 3 Kt-QB3, Kt-KB3; 4 B-Kt5, B-K2; 5 P-K3, O-O; 6 Kt-B3, QKt-Q2. Black observes the principles of simple development and works patiently to neutralise his opponent's initiative. 7 R-B1, P-B3; 8 B-Q3, PxP; 9 BxP, Kt-Q4; 10 BxB, QxB; 11 O-O, KtxKt; 12 RxKt, P-K4; 13 PxP, KtxP; 14 KtxKt, QxKt; 15 P-B4, Q-K5; 16 Q-K2, B-B4. Having safely brought out his Queen's Bishop, originally blocked in by the KP in this defence, Black may be said to have equalised.

(iv) **Tartakover Defence.** 2 . . . , P-K3; 3 Kt-QB3, Kt-KB3; 4 B-Kt5, B-K2; 5 P-K3, O-O; 6 Kt-B3, P-KR3; 7 B-R4, P-QKt3. In this case Black makes a different outlet for his awkward Bishop. 8 B-Q3, B-Kt2; 9 O-O, QKt-Q2; 10 R-B1, P-B4; 11 Q-K2, R-B1; 12 BPxP, KtxP; 13 BxB, QxB; 14 KtxKt, BxKt. Black's game is perfectly satisfactory.

(v) **Exchange Variation.** 2 . . . , P-K3; 3 Kt-QB3, Kt-KB3; 4 B-Kt5, QKt-Q2; 5 PxP. Thus White pins Black down to a more restricted defensive action. 5 . . . , PxP; 6 P-K3, P-B3; 7 B-Q3, B-K2; 8 Q-B2, Kt-B1; 9 Kt-B3, P-KKt3; 10 O-O, Kt-K3; 11 B-R4, O-O; 12 QR-Kt1, Kt-Kt2; 13 P-QKt4, B-KB4. Black has overcome the worst of his problems. (See diagram 101)

(vi) **Tarrasch Defence.** 2 . . . , P-K3; 3 Kt-QB3, P-QB4. Theoreticians are still undecided about this bold defence, in which Black stakes freedom of action against

101. Modern Queen's Gambit
This type of position is one
of the main reasons why the
classical methods of defending
the Queen's Gambit have
gradually declined in popularity. Black must exercise
great care on the Q side and
rarely obtains much counterplay on the other wing.

the isolation of his QP. 4 BPxP, KPxP; 5 Kt-B3, Kt-QB3;
6 P-KKt3, Kt-B3; 7 B-Kt2, B-K2; 8 O-O, O-O; 9 B-Kt5,
B-K3; 10 PxP, BxP; 11 R-B1, B-Kt3; 12 P-Kt3, R-K1.
White's position is the sounder.

(vii) **Semi-Tarrasch Defence.** 2 . . . , P-K3; 3 Kt-QB3,
Kt-KB3; 4 Kt-B3, P-B4. This counter-thrust is better
founded here, for Black can recapture on Q4 with a piece.
5 BPxP, KtxP; 6 P-K3, Kt-QB3; 7 B-Q3, B-K2; 8 O-O,
O-O; 9 P-QR3, PxP; 10 PxP, Kt-B3; 11 B-B2, P-QKt3;
12 Q-Q3, B-Kt2; 13 B-Kt5, P-Kt3. White's attacking
chances on the K side offset the weakness of his QP.

Colle System. 1 P-Q4, P-Q4; 2 Kt-KB3, Kt-KB3; 3 P-K3,
P-K3; 4 QKt-Q2, P-B4; 5 P-B3. Having stabilised the
position of his QP, White now plans to advance his KP.
5 . . . , QKt-Q2; 6 B-Q3, B-K2; 7 O-O, O-O; 8 P-K4,
QPxP; 9 KtxP, KtxKt; 10 BxKt, Kt-B3; 11 B-B2, P-QKt3.
Black has made use of his opponent's sedate manœuvres
to equalise completely.

Queen's Pawn, Budapest Defence. 1 P-Q4, Kt-KB3; 2
P-QB4, P-K4. Asymmetrical defences by nature enable
Black to impress his own strategy on the game. However,

this offer of a pawn for free play and some attacking propects is regarded as premature. 3 PxP, Kt-Kt5; 4 B-B4, Kt-QB3; 5 Kt-KB3, B-Kt5 ch; 6 QKt-Q2, Q-K2; 7 P-QR3, KKtxKP; 8 KtxKt, KtxKt; 9 P-K3, BxKt ch; 10 QxB, P-Q3; 11 B-K2, O-O; 12 O-O. White has returned the pawn to obtain two active Bishops.

Queen's Pawn, Nimzovitch Defence. 1 P-Q4, Kt-KB3; 2 P-QB4, P-K3; 3 Kt-QB3, B-Kt5. The pin continues the vital struggle for control of White's K4.

(i) 4 Q-B2—the Classical Variation, whereby White avoids the possibility of doubled QBPs and brings another piece to bear on K4. 4 . . . , P-Q4; 5 PxP, PxP; 6 B-Kt5, P-KR3; 7 BxKt, QxB; 8 P-QR3, BxKt ch; 9 QxB, O-O; 10 P-K3, P-B3; 11 Kt-B3, B-B4; 12 Kt-K5, Kt-Q2. Black completes his development without trouble.

(ii) 4 P-QR3—the Sämisch Variation, in which White invites the doubled pawns in order to establish a strong centre. 4 . . . , BxKt ch; 5 PxB, P-B4; 6 P-K3, O-O; 7 B-Q3, Kt-B3; 8 Kt-K2, P-QKt3; 9 P-K4, Kt-K1; 10 O-O, B-R3; 11 Q-R4, Q-B1; 12 B-K3, P-Q3; 13 QR-Q1, Kt-R4; 14 PxP, QPxP. White is restricted by his weakened pawn formation.

(iii) 4 P-K3, P-QKt3; 5 Kt-K2—the Rubinstein Variation, the basic idea of which is to enable White to secure the two Bishops without the doubling of his pawns. 5 . . . , B-R3; 6 P-QR3, BxKt ch; 7 KtxB, P-Q4; 8 P-QKt3, O-O; 9 B-K2, PxP; 10 PxP, Kt-B3; 11 P-QR4, Q-Q2; 12 Kt-Kt5, KR-Q1. Black is ahead in development and has active counterplay.

(iv) 4 P-K3, O-O; 5 B-Q3, P-B4; 6 Kt-B3, P-Q4; 7 O-O—the Modern Variation, which sees both sides building up their game along normal lines. 7 . . . , Kt-B3; 8 P-QR3, BxKt; 9 PxB, QPxP; 10 BxP, Q-B2 (see Diagram 102); 11 B-Q3, P-K4; 12 Q-B2, R-K1; 13 KtxP, KtxKt;

102. Key Theoretical Moment
The assessment of this situation is crucial for the whole defence. White again possesses the two Bishops, but Black can obtain good chances of the initiative by advancing his KP. Thorough practical testing has yet clearly to favour either side.

14 PxKt, QxP; 15 P-B3, B-Q2; 16 P-QR4, B-B3; 17 R-K1, QR-Q1. The position is delicately balanced.

Queen's Pawn, Queen's Indian Defence.   1 P-Q4, Kt-KB3; 2 P-QB4, P-K3; 3 Kt-KB3, P-QKt3. Here pressure on White's K4 square is to come from the fianchettoed Queen's Bishop.   4 P-KKt3, B-Kt2; 5 B-Kt2, B-K2; 6 O-O, O-O; 7 Kt-B3, Kt-K5; 8 Q-B2, KtxKt; 9 QxKt, P-KB4; 10 P-Kt3, B-KB3; 11 B-Kt2, P-Q3; 12 QR-Q1, Q-B1; 13 Q-Q2, B-K5; 14 Kt-K1, BxB; 15 KtxB, Kt-Q2; 16 Q-B2, Q-Kt2. The prospects are level.

Queen's Pawn, Modern Benoni Defence.   1 P-Q4, Kt-KB3; 2 P-QB4, P-B4; 3 P-Q5. The QP is provoked into advancing so that Black can retaliate in the centre and obtain counterplay with his King's Bishop on the KR1-QR8 diagonal.   3 . . . , P-K3; 4 Kt-QB3, PxP; 5 PxP, P-Q3; 6 Kt-B3, P-KKt3; 7 P-K4, B-Kt2; 8 B-K2, O-O; 9 O-O, R-K1; 10 Kt-Q2, Kt-R3; 11 P-B3. White has consolidated a small but definite spacial advantage.

Queen's Pawn, Old Indian Defence.   1 P-Q4, Kt-KB3; 2 P-QB4, P-Q3. Black prepares to advance his KP and contest the centre. 3 Kt-QB3, P-K4; 4 Kt-B3, QKt-Q2; 5 P-K4, B-K2; 6 B-K2, O-O; 7 O-O, P-B3; 8 Q-B2, R-K1; 9 R-Q1, B-B1; 10 R-Kt1. White remains in possession of the initiative.

Queen's Pawn, Grünfeld Defence. 1 P-Q4, Kt-KB3; 2 P-QB4, P-KKt3; 3 Kt-QB3, P-Q4. This is another provocative defence. Having permitted an enemy pawn centre to be formed, Black intends to attack it—with his fianchettoed King's Bishop in the forefront.

(i) 4 PxP—the Exchange Variation, the direct acceptance of the invitation. 4 . . . , KtxP; 5 P-K4, KtxKt; 6 PxKt, P-QB4; 7 B-QB4, B-Kt2; 8 Kt-K2, O-O; 9 O-O, PxP; 10 PxP, Kt-B3; 11 B-K3, B-Kt5; 12 P-B3, Kt-R4; 13 B-Q3, B-K3; 14 R-B1, BxRP; 15 P-Q5, B-Kt6; 16 Q-K1. White's powerful central build-up may balance the pawn sacrificed.

(ii) 4 P-K3—the Closed Variation, in which White is satisfied with a quiet formation. 4 . . . , B-Kt2; 5 Kt-B3, O-O; 6 B-K2, P-K3; 7 O-O, P-Kt3; 8 PxP, PxP; 9 P-QKt3, B-Kt2; 10 B-R3, R-K1; 11 R-B1, QKt-Q2; 12 B-Q3, R-QB1. Black has had no difficulty in equalising.

(iii) 4 Kt-B3, B-Kt2; 5 Q-Kt3—the Russian System, in which Black's strategy is subjected to its most searching examination. 5 . . . , PxP; 6 QxBP, O-O; 7 P-K4, B-Kt5; 8 B-K3, KKt-Q2; 9 B-K2, Kt-Kt3; 10 Q-B5, Kt-B3 (see Diagram 103); 11 P-Q5, Kt-Q2; 12 Q-R3, BxKt; 13 BxB, Kt-Q5; 14 O-O-O, KtxB; 15 PxKt. The white pawns are still standing.

Queen's Pawn, King's Indian Defence. 1 P-Q4, Kt-KB3; 2 P-QB4, P-KKt3; 3 Kt-QB3, B-Kt2. Black's policy here consists of flexible defence followed by counter-attack either on the K side or along the long black diagonal. Its dynamic, fighting character is fully in keeping with the modern approach.

103. Pawns versus Pieces
White has occupied the centre and established an advantage in space. However, Black has posted his pieces actively and is at present threatening to win the QP. The next few moves should decide whether the pawns or the pieces will emerge on top.

(i) 4 P-K4, P-Q3; 5 P-B4—the Four Pawns' Attack, an all-out effort to crush Black before he can hit back. 5 . . . , P-B4; 6 Kt-B3, O-O; 7 B-K2, PxP; 8 KtxP, Kt-B3; 9 B-K3, B-Kt5; 10 BxB, KtxB; 11 QxKt, KtxKt; 12 Q-Q1, Kt-B3; 13 R-QB1, Q-R4; 14 P-QR3, Q-R3; 15 Q-Q3, QR-B1. Black has sufficient counterplay.

(ii) 4 P-K4, P-Q3; 5 P-B3—the Sämisch Variation, in which White strengthens his pawn centre in preparation for a fierce onslaught on the King's wing. 5 . . . , O-O; 6 B-K3, P-K4; 7 P-Q5, P-B3; 8 Q-Q2, PxP; 9 BPxP, P-QR3; 10 P-KKt4, QKt-Q2; 11 KKt-K2, P-KR4; 12 P-KR3, Kt-R2; 13 PxP, Q-R5 ch; 14 B-B2, QxP(R5); 15 Kt-Kt3, Q-R3. By his bold response on the KR file Black has neutralised most of White's threats.

(iii) 4 P-K4, P-Q3; 5 Kt-B3, O-O; 6 B-K2, P-K4; 7 O-O —the Classical Variation, which usually leads to thematic play on opposite flanks. 7 . . . , Kt-B3; 8 P-Q5, Kt-K2; 9 Kt-K1, Kt-Q2; 10 Kt-Q3, P-KB4 (see Diagram 104); 11 PxP, KtxBP; 12 P-B3, Kt-B3; 13 Kt-B2, Kt-Q5; 14 KKt-K4, Kt-R4; 15 B-Kt5, Q-Q2; 16 P-KKt3, P-KR3; 17 B-K3. There is a sharp struggle ahead.

(iv) 4 P-KKt3, O-O; 5 B-Kt2, P-Q3; 6 Kt-B3, QKt-Q2; 7 O-O, P-K4—the Fianchetto Variation, in which White

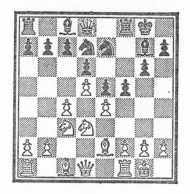

104. Dynamic Defence
The opposing pawn chains dictate that White should advance on the Queen's wing and Black on the King's. While Black is the more cramped, his plan needs less preparation; here his counter-action on the KB file is already in motion.

fortifies his King position before expanding in the centre. 8 P-K4, P-B3; 9 P-KR3, Q-Kt3; 10 R-K1, PxP; 11 KtxP, Kt-Kt5; 12 QKt-K2, KKt-K4; 13 P-Kt3, Kt-B4; 14 B-K3, P-QR4; 15 R-Kt1, R-K1; 16 R-KB1. The careful manœuvres undertaken by White have enabled him to consolidate his spacial advantage.

(v) 4 P-KKt3, O-O; 5 B-Kt2, P-Q3; 6 Kt-B3, P-B4—the Yugoslav Variation, by which Black aims to keep his King's Bishop's line of action unobstructed. 7 O-O, Kt-B3; 8 P-Q5, Kt-QR4; 9 Kt-Q2, P-QR3; 10 Q-B2, R-Kt1; 11 P-Kt3, P-QKt4; 12 B-Kt2, P-K3; 13 QPxP, BxP; 14 PxP, PxP; 15 QR-Q1. White can build up pressure against the enemy QP.

Queen's Pawn, Dutch Defence. 1 P-Q4, P-KB4. Black covers the opponent's K4 square and at the same time announces his aggressive intentions on the K side. The concept tends to be inflexible.

(i) 2 P-QB4, P-K3; 3 P-KKt3, Kt-KB3; 4 B-Kt2, B-K2; 5 Kt-KB3, O-O; 6 O-O, P-Q4—the Stonewall Variation, by which Black sets up a firm barrier of pawns across the centre. 7 Q-B2, P-B3; 8 QKt-Q2, Q-K1; 9 Kt-K5, QKt-Q2;

10 Kt-Q3, Kt-K5; 11 Kt-B3, Kt-Q3; 12 P-Kt3. White's control of K5 restricts Black greatly.

(ii) **2 P-QB4, P-K3; 3 P-KKt3, Kt-KB3; 4 B-Kt2, B-K2; 5 Kt-KB3, O-O; 6 O-O, P-Q3**—the Modern Variation, which gives Black a more resilient formation. **7 Kt-B3, Q-K1; 8 R-K1, Q-Kt3; 9 P-K4, KtxP; 10 KtxKt, PxKt; 11 RxP, Kt-B3; 12 Q-K2, B-B3; 13 B-Q2, P-K4; 14 PxP, PxP; 15 B-B3.** White has the pressure.

English. 1 P-QB4. The basic strategy initiated by this move consists of pressure on the white squares in the centre and along the long white diagonal. The opening is noted for its flexibility and the transpositional possibilities it affords.

(i) **1 . . . , P-K4; 2 Kt-QB3, Kt-KB3; 3 Kt-B3, Kt-B3; 4 P-Q4**—the Four Knights' Variation, whereby the central tension is released. **4 . . . , PxP; 5 KtxP, B-Kt5; 6 B-Kt5, P-KR3; 7 B-R4, BxKt ch; 8 PxB, P-Q3; 9 P-B3, O-O; 10 P-K4, Kt-K4; 11 B-K2, Kt-Kt3; 12 B-B2.** White's two Bishops and advantage in space compensate for his broken Q-side pawns.

(ii) **1 . . . , Kt-KB3; 2 Kt-QB3, P-K3; 3 P-K4**—the Mikenas Variation, an unusually sharp way for White to handle this opening. **3 . . . , P-Q4; 4 P-K5, P-Q5; 5 PxKt, PxKt; 6 KtPxP, QxP; 7 P-Q4, P-B4; 8 Kt-B3, PxP; 9 B-Kt5, Q-B4; 10 PxP, B-Kt5 ch; 11 B-Q2, BxB ch; 12 QxB, Kt-B3; 13 B-Q3, Q-QR4.** The prospects are even.

(iii) **1 . . . , P-QB4; 2 Kt-QB3, Kt-QB3; 3 P-KKt3, P-KKt3; 4 B-Kt2, B-Kt2**—the Symmetrical Variation, in which the second player follows a mirror strategy of his own on the black squares. **5 Kt-B3, Kt-B3; 6 O-O, O-O; 7 P-Q3, P-QR3; 8 P-QR3, R-Kt1; 9 R-Kt1, P-Q3; 10 P-QKt4, PxP; 11 PxP, P-QKt4; 12 PxP, PxP; 13 B-Q2, B-Q2.** White's initiative is petering out.

Réti. **1 Kt-KB3, P-Q4; 2 P-B4.** The object of this hypermodern opening is likewise to preserve a flexible position and to control the centre from the flank—here the fianchetto of the Queen's Bishop is thematic. **2 . . . ,** **P-QB3; 3 P-QKt3, Kt-B3; 4 P-Kt3, B-B4; 5 B-KKt2, P-K3; 6 B-Kt2, QKt-Q2; 7 O-O, P-KR3; 8 P-Q3, B-K2; 9 QKt-Q2, O-O; 10 P-QR3, P-QR4; 11 Q-B2, B-R2; 12 B-B3, P-QKt4; 13 PxKtP, PxP; 14 P-QKt4, Q-B2.** Black's classical deployment of his pieces has brought a comfortable equality.

Catalan System. **1 Kt-KB3, Kt-KB3; 2 P-B4, P-K3; 3 P-KKt3, P-Q4; 4 P-Q4.** Here the long white diagonal is the axis of the struggle. **4 . . . , B-K2; 5 B-Kt2, O-O; 6 O-O, QKt-Q2; 7 Q-B2, P-B3; 8 P-QKt3, P-QKt3; 9 B-Kt2, B-Kt2; 10 Kt-B3, R-B1; 11 QR-Q1, Q-B2; 12 P-K4.** Black is hard pressed to maintain his ground in the centre.

King's Indian Attack. **1 Kt-KB3, Kt-KB3; 2 P-KKt3, P-Q4; 3 B-Kt2, P-B4; 4 O-O, Kt-B3; 5 P-Q3, P-K3; 6 QKt-Q2, B-K2; 7 P-K4.** White's general plan is to establish his pawn at K5 and use the extra space on the K side to work up an attack. **7 . . . , O-O; 8 R-K1, Q-B2; 9 P-K5, Kt-Q2; 10 Q-K2, P-QKt4; 11 Kt-B1, P-QR4; 12 P-KR4, B-R3; 13 B-B4, P-Kt5.** Black has counterplay on the Queen's wing.

Bird. **1 P-KB4.** White combines flank control with K-side aggression. **1 . . . , P-Q4; 2 Kt-KB3, Kt-KB3; 3 P-K3, P-KKt3; 4 P-QKt3, B-Kt2; 5 B-Kt2, O-O; 6 B-K2, P-B4; 7 O-O, Kt-B3; 8 Kt-K5, Q-B2; 9 KtxKt, QxKt; 10 B-KB3, B-K3; 11 P-Q3, Q-Q2.** The game is about level.

Sokolsky. 1 P-QKt4. This eccentric move is designed to secure an immediate advantage in space on the Q side. 1 . . . , Kt-KB3; 2 B-Kt2, P-Q4; 3 P-K3, P-K3; 4 P-Kt5, P-B4; 5 Kt-KB3, B-Q3; 6 P-B4, QKt-Q2; 7 B-K2, O-O; 8 O-O (see Diagram 105), Q-K2; 9 P-QR4, P-K4; 10

105. Opening of the Future
White's formation is an extreme illustration of the constant search for greater flexibility in opening play. His K-side pawns are left largely untouched; his central options are reserved; only on the Queen's wing does he commit himself to an early action.

PxP, P-K5; 11 Kt-K1, KtxP; 12 P-Q3, PxP; 13 KtxP, QKt-B3. Black has equalised by countering in the centre.

6

MIDDLEGAME PLANNING

As soon as the two sides have developed most of their men the opening may be said to be over and the game enters its second and middle phase. It is here that the real struggle takes place: the opposing forces settle down in earnest to the tasks of attack and defence or of manœuvring for an advantage, and in the majority of cases this is where the final outcome is decided.

The 'middlegame' does not have its own detailed theory; for the basic positions to be analysed are too numerous and complex. What is known about it has grown out of the games and writings of experts and is expressed almost entirely in terms of concepts and themes. The player cannot therefore expect this generalised knowledge to provide him with the right move at any given moment; he must use it as a guide, relating it to the specific characteristics of the situation before him to work out a strategic plan.. The better the plan corresponds to the position the more easily the individual moves fit into place.

Uncastled King

The most primitive type of middlegame campaign arises when one player does not pay proper attention to the needs of development and is subjected to an attack before he has castled. In the position in Diagram 106, for example, White is poised for action, whereas Black's force is as yet unco-ordinated. To exploit his advantage White needs only to open up attacking lines for his pieces—they will do the rest! Black, on the other hand, if he is to have

106. King in Peril
Black's King is still on its original square, he has only two pieces in active play and his pawn formation has been compromised. A breakthrough by White followed by a powerful assault down the centre and KB files is imminent.

any hope of survival, must strive to block the centre and use the breathing-space to organise some sort of defence. Accordingly, 1 . . . , P-K4 is the correct move.

In the game in which this position occurred, however, Black played the 'aggressive' **1 . . . , P-Q4**, quite disregarding the fact this sharpens the central conflict rather than blunts it. As White was quick to demonstrate, the threat to the Bishop is meaningless strategically. The continuation was: **2 BPxP, BPxP** (if 2 . . . , PxB, then 3 PxP ch, KxP; 4 KR-B1, winning the Queen); **3 KR-B1, Q-Kt2; 4 PxP, BPxP; 5 BxQP** (White willingly gives up the piece to lay bare the enemy King), .PxB; **6 QxQP, B-Q2; 7 KR-K1 ch** (it is now just a matter of tactics), **K-Q1; 8 R-Q4** (threatening Q-R5 ch followed by R-B4 ch), **R-Kt3; 9 Q-R8 ch, Resigns.** White's planning triumphed: at the end Black was still trying to surmount problems that belong to the opening.

King's-Side Attack
While castling is the routine way of avoiding fiascos on the K file, it is far from always safe for the King on the flanks. Direct attacks are by no means ruled out, and in some circumstances a player may regret that he did not

think again before moving his King. Such must have been the case in the position shown in Diagram 107. Having

107. Impending Attack
By advancing his KBP to the fifth rank White has secured a spacial advantage on the K side and laid the foundations for an attack. As the KRP has already been ·moved, Black's King position now lacks some of its defensive resilience.

been given early warning of enemy aggression on the K side, Black prudently put off castling there. But at length he lost patience and chanced it. Now, realising how difficult a campaign of defensive manœuvring would be, he decided to try to break White's grip immediately and played **1 . . . , P-Q4.** After **2 KtxQP, KtxKt; 3 PxKt, QxQP** a casual glance might suggest that the plan had succeeded, but the reply **4 P-B6** destroys any illusions. This thrust leads inevitably to the collapse of Black's King position.

Play continued: **4 . . . , KR-K1; 5 R-R4, R-K3; 6 Kt-Q2, K-R2; 7 R-KKt4, R-KKt1; 8 Kt-K4** (the fluency with which the white pieces combine in the attack is worth studying), **K-R1** (White was threatening 9 Kt-Kt5 ch, PxKt; 10 Q-R3 ch, K-Kt3; 11 RxP ch, KxR; 12 R-B5 ch, K-Kt3; 13 Q-R5 mate—a fine illustration of the way correct planning generates tactical solutions); **9 P-B3** (preventing Black from exchanging Queens by . . . , Q-Q5), **Q-Q1; 10 Kt-Kt5** (White forces the win of material, keeping up the pressure into the bargain), **RxP; 11 KtxP ch, RxKt; 12 RxR, Q-Q3; 13 Q-Kt3, P-KKt4; 14 Q-B2, R-Kt2; 15**

R-B8 ch, K-R2; 16 Q-B5 ch, Q-Kt3; 17 Q-B8, Resigns (the threat of R-R8 ch is too strong). Once the conditions were favourable for attack White did not miss a single opportunity.

Castling on Opposite Wings.

If it is necessary to throw forward more than one pawn in order to breach the enemy defences, one's own King may prove better placed on the other wing; for then it is possible to undertake an all-out onslaught without the risk of weakening its position and inviting a sudden counter-attack. However, there are two sides to every coin, and the player who stations his King on the Queen's wing when his opponent's is on the King's (or *vice versa*) must recognise the fact that he may himself be setting up a target for storming operations. Moreover, if he commits his forces too eagerly to the flank action, he is liable to lose his footing in the centre—and the attacker can rarely afford that.

This type of middlegame is frequently likened to a race, with victory going to him who can first force open attacking lines in front of the enemy King. Its tense, double-edged situations call for good nerves and a readiness to take bold decisions, some of them sacrificial ones. The continuation from the position in Diagram 108 illustrates how many of the typical problems that come up should be tackled.

After White had set the pace with 1 P-KKt4, K-R1; 2 QR-Kt1 Black responded with the equally energetic 2 . . . . , P-Kt4; 3 BxKt, KtxB; 4 P-Kt5, Kt-K5; 5 KtxKt, PxKt; 6 BxKP, B-K3. By giving up a pawn he was able to contain the first wave of the assault and create threats of his own on the Q side. The game was now at a very critical point; for if White's plans were to succeed, he had to find a method of breaking through quickly. This he

108. Both Sides must Attack
White castled Q side expressly to launch a full-scale offensive (employing both pawns and pieces) against his opponent's King. In self-defence Black must hit back at the white King, even though he is not particularly well placed for doing so.

did with **7 P-Kt6,** which at one stroke clears the way for the Rook on KKt1 and frees the KKt5 square for his Knight. The idea would never have occurred to White if he had not been thinking along the right strategic lines.

Play went on: **7 . . . , RPxP; 8 Kt-Kt5, P-KB4** (his defences would otherwise be smashed by BxKtP); **9 KtxB, RxKt; 10 B-B3** (10 BxQBP, R-QB1; 11 P-Q5, R-K5, when Black has counterplay, would quite contradict the theme of K-side attack), **R-QB1; 11 P-KR4, P-B4; 12 P-Q5** (he naturally wants to keep the QB file closed), **R-B3; 13 P-R5, P-Kt4; 14 RxP, P-QB5; 15 K-Kt1, QR-B1; 16 KR-Kt1, QR-B2; 17 R-Kt6, B-K4; 18 P-R6** (the crowning blow of the campaign: Black's pawn cover is finally breached), **PxP; 19 R-Kt8 ch, K-R2; 20 B-R5, R-B1; 21 RxR, RxR; 22 P-B4, B-Kt2; 23 B-Kt6 ch, K-R1; 24 BxP, Q-B4; 25 Q-Kt2, Q-K2; 26 Q-Kt6.** The end is near. Black parted with the exchange by 26 . . . , RxB but resigned six moves later.

Queen's-Side Majority

Direct attack on the King may be the simplest type of plan in the middlegame, but it is certainly not the only type. Indeed, improved standards of defensive technique have caused masters to avoid 'playing for mate' unless the conditions definitely favour it and, instead, to cultivate less committal methods of exploiting an advantage. The logical setting for these alternatives is the Q side, where a player is generally free to pursue an initiative without too great danger of overreaching himself. If, therefore, he has a preponderance or 'majority' of pawns (e.g. 4 to 3) on that part of the board, he can often develop its potential as an attacking weapon to the full.

The position in Diagram 109 is the result of some tame

109. Birth of a Majority
By advancing his QBP to the fifth rank Black can set up a Q-side majority of 3 to 2 (i.e. QRP, QKtP and QBP versus QRP and QKtP). This numerical superiority should eventually enable him to create a passed pawn by force.

opening play by White (in particular, the manœuvre B-Q2-K1). Black has been permitted not only to complete his development easily but also to expand on the Queen's wing. Now he must decide how to make use of what he has achieved. Attacking the white king is pointless, since it is securely guarded; while a routine move such as . . . , KR-Q1 would allow White to ease his game by PxP. Black's right course is to press on with his Q-side pawns, using them to repulse his opponent's pieces and provide his own with even more manœuvring room. It is true that White's QP is thereby left in uncontested occupation of the centre, but without the initiative this carries insufficient weight.

108

Play went as follows: **1 . . . , P-B5; 2 B-B2, P-Kt5; 3 Kt-Kt1, Q-Kt4; 4 QKt-Q2, KR-B1; 5 Kt-B1, P-QR4; 6 Kt-Kt3, B-R3; 7 P-K4, P-R5; 8 B-Q2** (after this passive move the black pawns have a completely smooth run; White should at least have tried for some counterplay by 8 P-Q5), **P-Kt6; 9 PxP, BPxP; 10 QxQ, BxQ; 11 B-Kt1, P-R6; 12 PxP, P-Kt7** (the climax of Black's strategy: on the brink of promotion, the QKtP cripples all resistance and soon forces material gains); **13 R-R2, BxP; 14 P-K5, Kt-Q4; 15 Kt-K4, B-B5; 16 RxB, RxR; 17 Kt-Q6, R-B2; 18 Kt-KKt5, B-Q6; 19 R-K1, BxB; 20 Kt-Kt5, R-R8; 21 KtxR, B-B4; 22 KtxKt, RxR ch; 23 BxR, P-Kt8=Q; 24 Kt-K7 ch, K-B1; Resigns.** White could well have surrendered earlier but was reluctant to concede the pawn majority such a crushing victory.

Minority Attack

Paradoxical though it may seem, a pawn 'minority' may also be advanced with aggressive intent. The idea in this case is not to overpower the enemy pawns—that is hardly feasible—but to draw the majority's sting before it has the chance to roll into action. The 'minority attack' is most effective when the opposing pawns have already lost some of their flexibility, as illustrated in Diagram 110.

Black would have reasonable prospects if he could work up a counter-attack in the centre and on the K side, but by falling slightly behind in development he has let the first player's initiative become too strong. With **1 P-Kt5** White immediately turned on the pressure, not even pausing to advance his QRP (that is only necessary if . . . , P-QR3 has been played). No matter how Black replies now, he cannot avoid compromising his defences.

The game continued: **1 . . . , B-Q2; 2 PxP, BxP** (2 . . . , PxP leaves him with a weak QBP); **3 Q-Kt3, B-K2; 4 QBxKt, BxB; 5 B-Kt5, Q-Q3; 6 KR-B1, P-KR4** (a des-

110. Advancing a Minority
Black's sound but defensively rigid formation on the Q side invites attack from the enemy minority. The plan for White, well under way here, consists in playing P-QKt5, weakening the black pawns and creating threats on the QKt and QB files.

perate attempt to stir up trouble in the vicinity of the white King); **7** Kt-K2, P-R5; **8** BxB, PxB (it is some consolation to Black to be rid of his useless Queen's Bishop); **9** Q-R4, Kt-K2; **10** R-Kt7, P-R4; **11** P-KR3, KR-Kt1; **12** KR-Kt1, RxR; **13** RxR, P-B4 (advancing the pawns now merely accentuates their weakness); **14** R-Kt5, PxP; **15** QKtxP, R-QB1; **16** Kt-Kt3, B-B6; **17** QxKRP (the first gain for White; more soon follow), R-B5; **18** P-Kt4, P-R5; **19** QKt-Q4, BxKt; **20** KtxB, Q-K4; **21** Kt-B3, Q-Q3; **22** R-R5, R-B1 (R-R8 ch was threatened); **23** RxRP, Kt-Kt3; **24** Q-R5, Q-KB3; **25** Q-B5, Q-B3; **26** R-R7, R-B1; **27** R-Q7, P-Q5; **28** RxQP. Being three pawns down, Black resigned within a couple of moves. White handled the minority attack in classic style, wearing the opposition down by unspectacular yet insistent threats. Towards the end Black's ragged position simply fell to pieces.

Colour Complexes

Many middlegame situations arise in which neither attacking breakthroughs nor general strategic advances are suitable. Instead, the whole campaign may revolve around a static weakness that can only be exploited by skilful manœuvres with the pieces. When, for instance, a player is left with a backward pawn his opponent's efforts naturally tend to be concentrated in its direction. The pawn itself is a permanent liability, but often it is accompanying weak squares which prove the most harmful to the defence. Thus, in the position shown in Diagram 111

111. Black-Square Strategy
White's unassailable Knight is the key piece in his plan. Its domination of the board will prevent the opposition from undertaking anything effective and so make it easier for White to carry out a gradual invasion on the weakened black squares.

as well as the 'hole' at K4 the points on each side of the KP, Black's Q3 and KB3, lack pawn protection; furthermore, this 'complex' of black squares can be extended to include KR3, KKt4 and QB4, all of which are to a greater or lesser degree vulnerable to attack.

The last straw for Black here is his feeble or, as it is usually called, 'bad' Bishop. Whereas a Knight or a Bishop operating on black squares could offer real resistance to white invaders, it is of little use in this respect; severely hampered by its own pawns, it is doomed to almost total inactivity for the rest of the game.

The first stage of White's plan consists in driving off the enemy Queen and posting his Rooks more aggressively. This he accomplished as follows: **1 Q-KB2, P-KKt4; 2 PxP, RxKtP; 3 P-R3, Q-K2; 4 QR-B1, R-Kt2; 5 Q-K3, B-R4; 6 K-R3, Q-B3; 7 P-KKt4, B-K1; 8 K-Kt3, Q-Q1; 9 R-KR1, Q-Kt3; 10 R-R2, Q-Q1; 11 R-R6, Q-Q3;**

12 K-Kt2, B-Kt3; 13 R-B5, Q-Kt3; 14 Q-B3, Q-Q1; 15 Q-B1. Now Black is entirely on the defensive; he cannot stop the slow infiltration of White's major pieces.

Play went on: **15 . . . , Q-B3; 16 R-B8, Q-K2; 17 RxR ch, QxR; 18 R-R1, Q-Q1; 19 Q-R6, Q-Q3; 20 Q-B4, Q-Kt3; 21 R-QB1, Q-Q1** (the threats on his back rank did not allow him time to take the QKtP); **22 K-Kt3, B-K1; 23 Q-R6, B-Kt3; 24 R-B3, Q-KB1; 25 Q-B1, B-K1; 26 R-B8, R-K2; 27 Q-Kt5 ch, K-R1; 28 Kt-Q3** (that White can afford to retire his beautifully placed Knight is proof how much he is on top; Black is in a stranglehold), **Q-Kt2; 29 Q-R5, Q-B1; 30 Q-K5 ch, Q-Kt2; 31 Q-Kt8, Q-B1; 32 QxRP, P-R4; 33 Q-Kt8, PxP; 34 PxP, K-R2; 35 R-B7, P-Kt4; 36 Kt-B4, K-Kt1; 37 RxR, QxR; 38 Q-K5, K-B2; 39 P-Kt5, B-Q2; 40 P-Kt6 ch, Resigns** (if **40 . . . , K-Kt1,** then **41 KtxQP**). It is instructive that White made no attempt to win the backward KP; control of his K5 square plus the run of its related weak points was far more important.

Obviously, such a complex may just as well be comprised of white squares, and in that case all the colour roles are the opposite of those in the above example. The black-squared Bishop would then be the one liable to be hemmed in by the pawns and therefore to cut a poor figure throughout the campaign.

Strategic Defence

A capacity for stiff resistance when in difficulties is one of the most valuable qualities a player can possess. In practice, to have made a mistake and got into a bad position does not mean that defeat is inevitable. By recognising the danger and applying the normal principles of strategy it is often possible either to stem the tide and secure equality or to create so many problems for the opponent that he lets slip his advantage himself. The continuation from Diagram 112 shows what can be achieved by the full use of defensive resources.

112. White under Pressure
White is hard pressed across his entire front: his King position has been compromised; the Q file is at present in Black's hands; finally, his QKtP is threatened by the raking enemy Bishop. The defensive tasks before White are enormous.

White began his rearguard action with **1 Kt-Kt3, Kt-B5; 2 R-Q1,** leaving his QKtP to its fate in order to challenge the enemy Rook. After **2 . . . , RxR; 3 QxR, BxP; 4 Q-R4, B-Kt2; 5 Q-K8 ch, K-R2; 6 Q-K4 ch, Kt-Kt3; 7 Kt-R5, Q-B8 ch; 8 K-R2, Q-B3; 9 Q-Q3, Q-B2 ch; 10 K-R1, B-R1; 11 Q-K4, Q-B8 ch; 12 K-R2, Q-B2 ch; 13 K-R1, Q-B2; 14 Q-B2** he was clearly beginning to breathe more freely: by exploiting his one trump, a grip on the white squares on the K side, he had managed to obtain some counterplay. But his troubles were not over; for Black now had an extra pawn up his sleeve.

Play went on: **14 . . . , P-Kt4; 15 Q-B6, P-Kt5; 16 Kt-Kt3, QxP; 17 Q-Kt7 ch, B-Kt2; 18 Kt-B5, Q-R8 ch; 19 K-R2, Q-B3; 20 QxRP, P-Kt6; 21 Q-Kt7, P-Kt7; 22 Kt (B3)-Q4** (cutting the QKtP off from protection and thus bringing the draw within sight), **Kt-K4; 23 QxP, KtxP ch; 24 K-R3, Q-K4; 25 P-Kt3, Q-K5; 26 Q-QB2** (as on the move before, when capturing the Knight was playable, White takes the safe line: 26 KtxB, Kt-K6 would have given Black further chances), **QxQ; 27 KtxQ, P-R4; 28 Kt(B2)-K3, KtxKt; 29 KtxKt.** The game was agreed drawn a few moves later, since White was ready to part with his Knight to thwart the black pawns—heroic defence to the last.

Even Positions

The most difficult conditions in which to find an appropriate plan are those where neither side enjoys any advantage. It may be easy enough if there are mutual targets for attack (i.e. a situation of 'dynamic balance'), but positions that have few distinctive features (the symmetrical type, for instance) yet are still tense can present very awkward problems. The essence of it is that the player feels in a dilemma: he would like to take positive measures but is afraid lest he commit himself to something that cannot be completed.

What then is the correct policy in circumstances where forcing actions are not justified? The answer is that one must 'manœuvre'; for only by manœuvring is it possible to progress while standing still, so to speak. The pieces are transferred to better posts and key points are strengthened, all with the aim of securing a harmonious, flexible position in which the forces can co-operate actively and respond to whatever calls are made on them. That is middlegame planning at its deepest, and for practical examples the reader is asked to consult the games in Chapter 8.

7

ENDGAME THEORY AND PRACTICE

The basic situations upon which all theoretical knowledge ultimately depends were analysed in Chapter 2; here the range is extended to endings in the more general sense of the word. Inevitably, since the field is so vast, but a tiny fraction of the available material can be included. However, all the most important types of ending are covered, and the picture has been completed by a selection of characteristic examples taken from practical play.

Because the endgame is by nature simpler than the opening or middlegame (there are not so many men on the board), it is a sharper test of a player's ability. Errors are not only less frequently overlooked but they now have a greater finality. As a result, the third and last phase of the game has acquired a fearsome reputation, and it is not uncommon even for experts to go out of their way to avoid exchanges and the transition to a particular ending; though aware that that would be the logical method of following up their middlegame manoeuvres, they prefer to chance their luck in artificially contrived complications. It need hardly be said that this is a narrow, self-defeating attitude and not to be recommended to anyone. The endgame shows up faults, it is true, but its clear light also provides the best conditions for observing the principles of chess at work. He who neglects it, therefore, misses a golden opportunity of improving his all-round skill.

Queen versus Rook

The powers of the various pieces are seen in bright relief

113. Superiority of the Queen
Being overpowered by the Queen, Black is obliged to retreat step by step to the edge of the board.

in endings where they meet in final combat, lone survivors of the bloodshed. In such circumstances, with the whole board at its command, the Queen is irresistible. It has no trouble dealing with the minor pieces, and only in the Rook does it find a serious opponent. In fact, the Rook is sometimes able to exploit stalemate to force a draw, but this is an exception and arises because the stronger side's men obstruct each other.

The normal winning process consists in driving the King and Rook into one of the corners, where they run out of manœuvring space. From the position shown in Diagram 113 play continues: **1 Q-B6 ch, K-K1; 2 Q-R8 ch, K-B2; 3 Q-B8, R-K2 ch** (the alternative is 3 . . . , K-K2; 4 Q-KKt8, R-B2; 5 Q-Kt7 ch, K-Q1; 6 Q-B8 ch, K-Q2; 7 K-Q5, R-Kt2, when Black is gradually forced into his right-hand corner); **4 K-B5, K-Kt2; 5 Q-Q8, R-B2 ch; 6 K-Kt5, K-R2; 7 Q-Q4, R-Kt2 ch; 8 K-B6, K-Kt1; 9 Q-Q8 ch, K-R2; 10 Q-K8.**

A so-called '*Zugzwang*' position has now been reached (this is a German term made up from *Zug*—'move' and *zwingen*—'to compel')—the moment of truth for the defending forces. A typical finish would be: **10 . . . ,**

114. Black is in Zugzwang
He is compelled to move his Rook away from the protection of the King (10 . . . , R-Kt1, for example, would allow 11 Q-R5 mate); the consequences are fatal.

R-Kt8; 11 Q-K4 ch, K-Kt1; 12 Q-R8 ch, K-R2; 13 Q-R7 ch and 14 QxR.

Although the concept of *Zugzwang* does occasionally appear in the earlier stages of the game, its main role is reserved for the endgame. Loosely related to stalemate, it does much the same for the attacker as that device does for the defender.

Rook versus Minor Piece

The Rook makes all the running against either Bishop or Knight, but it cannot force a win unless the weaker side's pieces are badly placed or the defence is mishandled. If the defender has a Bishop, his simplest course is to retreat at once with his King to a corner square of the colour that the Bishop does not control, as illustrated in Diagram 115. After 1 K-R6, B-R7; 2 R-R7, B-Kt6; 3 R-R8 ch,

115. King in a Safe Corner
Black's position is unassailable; for while his King stays where it is the Bishop can always meet checks by interposing at either KKt1 or KR2.

B-Kt1 White has a choice between withdrawing his Rook and giving stalemate. It is a draw.

The ending of Knight versus Rook is more difficult to defend, since the Knight's mobility decreases sharply as it gets near to the corners. The safest plan is to keep King and Knight in close co-operation and to take up a back-to-the-wall position like that in Diagram 116. Play might then continue: 1 K-Q6, Kt-B2 ch; 2 K-K6, Kt-Q1 ch; 3 K-B6, K-B1; 4 R-Q7, K-K1; 5 R-K7 ch, K-B1; 6 R-K1, Kt-Kt2; 7 K-K6, K-K1; 8 R-QKt1, Kt-Q1 ch; 9 K-Q6, Kt-B2 ch; 10 K-K6, Kt-Q1 ch, and White has no more than a draw.

117

116. The Defence Holds
Black has permitted himself
to be driven back into a
defensive position which he
knows cannot be broken
down.

Queen versus Pawn

A pawn is no match for a piece if the conditions are level,
but when it is in sight of promotion and supported by the
King even the Queen dare not take the result for granted.
Indeed, should the enemy have already reached the seventh
rank, as in Diagram 117, the Queen is normally certain of

117. Conquest of a KtP
White forces the black King
to block the pawn's path,
thereby gaining time to bring
his own King into action.

victory against only a KtP, QP or KP. The win (sometimes
a rather protracted affair) is accomplished in the above
position as follows: 1 Q-K6 ch, K-R6; 2 Q-K4, K-R7; 3
Q-R4 ch, K-Kt8 (now White is free to move his King);
4 K-Kt2, K-B8; 5 Q-QB4 ch, K-Q7; 6 Q-Kt6, K-B8; 7
Q-B3 ch, K-Kt8 (the process has been repeated); 8 K-B2,
K-R7; 9 Q-B2, K-R8; 10 Q-R4 ch, K-Kt8; 11 K-K2, K-B8;
12 Q-Q1 mate.

In the case of a RP or BP the stronger side is baulked
by stalemate and is therefore unable to win unless its King
is already near enough to help construct a mating finish.
A typical draw is shown in Diagram 118: after 1 Q-Kt4 ch,
K-B7; 2 Q-R3, K-Kt8; 3 Q-Kt3 ch, K-R1 the white Queen
must concede the pawn its due. For what would happen
in the same circumstances to a BP the reader is asked to

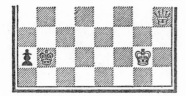

118. White cannot Win
It is impossible for White to gain time by driving the King into the corner, as it is then stalemated.

turn back to Diagram 14—it just leaves itself to be captured.

Rook versus Pawn

The prospects for the player with the pawn are much better here, since the Rook does not command the Queen's ability to bring the pawn to a permanent stop simply by occuping a square in front of it. If the pawn is escorted by the King while the Rook lacks ready support, the stronger side may be unable to win even though the pawn is still in its own half of the board.

There is practically no limit to the different situations which may be encountered, but all of them, fortunately, can be resolved on the same principle as that illustrated in Diagram 119. The major question in this instance is

119. General Test for Success
White wins if both King and Rook can control a square which the pawn has yet to pass over.

whether the white King can circumvent its opposite number and catch the pawn before or as it queens. Analysis show that this is possible—given precise play: **1 K-Q6, P-Kt5; 2 K-Q5, K-B5; 3 K-Q4, K-B6; 4 K-Q3, P-Kt6; 5 R-B7 ch** (forcing the black King to block the pawn), **K-Kt7; 6 K-K2, K-R7; 7 K-B3, P-Kt7; 8 R-R7 ch, K-Kt8; 9 R-KKt7,**

K-R8 (setting a last trap: 10 RxP stalemate); **10 K-B2,** and the pawn falls.

If it were Black's move in the above position, the result would be a draw. White would be too late to overhaul the advancing pawn with his King and so would have to sacrifice the Rook for it. A single tempo decides everything.

Minor Piece versus Pawn

Since a minor piece is not powerful enough to mate a lone King, the roles of the two sides are reversed in this type of ending and it is the player with the piece who as a rule must aim for the draw. In most cases he has no trouble, as the piece gives itself up if necessary. However, a Knight may find this difficult when compelled to deal single-handed with both an advanced pawn and the enemy King. As opposed to a Bishop, which can observe the situation from afar, it needs to be able to manœuvre in the close vicinity of the pawn.

A RP is the most awkward. In order to deal with one, the Knight has to halt it on the sixth rank by controlling the square in front, as shown in Diagram 120. After

120. Defensive Pirouette
By turning about on the squares QB1, QR2, QKt4 and Q3 the Knight holds off both King and pawn.

1 . . . , K-Q7; 2 Kt-R2 (but not 2 Kt-Kt3 ch, K-B7; 3 Kt-Q4 ch, K-Kt7, when the Knight is helpless to stop the pawn), K-B7; 3 K-Kt3, K-Kt7; 4 Kt-Kt4, K-Kt6; 5 Kt-Q3, K-B6 (or 5 . . . , P-R7; 6 Kt-B1 ch and 7 KtxP); 6 Kt-B1, K-Kt7; 7 Kt-Q3 ch, K-B7; 8 Kt-Kt4 ch, K-B6; 9 Kt-R2 ch the game is clearly drawn.

A pawn on any other file may be allowed to reach the seventh rank without the result being affected; for the extra manœuvring room at the Knight's disposal enables it to maintain the blockade from the queening square. The resourcefulness of the Knight is never to be denied.

Pawn Promotion

The greatest distinguishing feature of the endgame is the changed role of the pawns. As the pieces disappear from the board and the King has less and less need of cover the pawns become powerful in their own right. With fewer defensive duties to fulfil, they are much more at liberty to advance whenever and wherever the opportunity arises. Consequently, promotion is transformed from the rather rare event that it is in the middlegame into a natural strategic task.

Before a player can expect to queen a pawn by force he must, generally speaking, possess a definite advantage; otherwise the defence will surely beat off the attempt. A pawn is the obvious unit of measurement, and a large part of endgame theory is devoted to the analysis of the problems facing the two sides when one is a pawn ahead. The assumption is that the pawn is not enough in itself to win the game: it must be exploited to gain more material (e.g. a piece), which in turn can be used either to make further gains or to enforce mate directly. If this is impossible, a draw results.

Rook and Pawn versus Rook

As each exchange of pawns inexorably lessens the opponent's chances of queening, it is a matter of fundamental technique in all endings for the weaker side to strive for relief in this way. When every pawn except one has been exchanged (in other words, the defender has carried this policy of elimination to its logical conclusion)

121

the effect of the extra material is reduced to a minimum: the sought-after draw is as near as it theoretically can be.

If each player has a minor piece, to reach safety it is only necessary to give up the piece for the pawn—which should not be too difficult a task. Where major pieces are concerned it is a different story. Then there is normally no question of a sacrifice to end the pawn's career; a permanent blockade is required. The ideal defensive position in the case of Rook and pawn versus Rook is illustrated in Diagram 121. To get anywhere White must try **1 P-K6**

121. A Standard Draw
Black's King firmly bars the pawn's way to its queening square, while his Rook holds off the white King.

(intending to create a mating threat by K-Q6), but after **1 . . . , R-R8; 2 K-Q6, R-Q8 ch; 3 K-K5, R-K8 ch; 4 K-B6, R-B8 ch** the game is patently drawn. The point to note is that the defending Rook does not leave the third rank until the pawn provides the enemy King with some cover there.

The methods of play when the King is unable to block the pawn's path (it may be cut off by the enemy Rook, for instance) are invariably too complex to be examined outside specialised works on the endgame. Here the reader must be content with the advice that he keep his Rook as active as possible—while it thrives he will thrive.

Queen and Pawn versus Queen

So numerous are the possibilities open to two Queens on an almost empty board that this ending defies exhaustive analysis. If the pawn is not far advanced or is opposed by the King, a draw usually follows. But in other cases the mass of impenetrable variations heavily handicaps the defender, for whom a single slip may be fatal.

Once the pawn has reached the seventh rank—not something one ought to rely upon achieving, of course— the stronger side's prospects of winning are very much enhanced. The continuation from the position in Diagram 122 is a fine example of the techniques involved. **1 K-R7,**

122. Breaking the Defence
White manœuvres his King and Queen in order to unpin the pawn in a situation where Black's checks run out.

Q-B6; 2 K-Kt7, Q-B6 ch; 3 K-Kt8, Q-B5; 4 Q-Kt2 ch, K-R2; 5 Q-B2 ch, K-Kt2; 6 Q-B3 ch, K-R2; 7 K-R7, Q-B7 ch; 8 K-Kt7, Q-QKt7 ch; 9 K-Kt8, Q-QR7; 10 Q-K4, Q-Kt6; 11 Q-Q4 ch, K-R1; 12 Q-R1 ch, K-Kt2; 13 Q-K5 (White's Queen is now in a commanding position; Black's has correspondingly less scope and cannot maintain the defence for many more moves), Q-B5; 14 K-Kt7, Q-Kt5 ch; 15 K-B6, Q-R5 ch; 16 K-K6, Q-Kt5 ch; 17 K-K7, Q-Kt5 ch; 18 K-K8, Q-R5 ch; 19 K-Q8, Q-R1 ch; 20 K-K7, Q-R6 ch; 21 Q-Q6, Q-K6 ch; 22 K-Q8, and the pawn promotes.

Practical Endings
When the number of pawns left is comparatively large— which is the case at the outset of most endings—the theoretical aspect remains in the background. Detailed knowledge tells the player what to aim for, but the actual play must be conducted on broadly the same basis of commonsense as in the preceding stages of the game. To put it another way, though the endgame raises peculiar problems, there is no conflict with general concepts like

123

command of space and co-operation of the forces; given proper attention, they still provide the surest formula for success. This simple truth is all too poorly appreciated, yet it is proved again and again in practice.

Pawn Endings

Where the only 'officers' left alive are the Kings an extra pawn is nearly always a decisive advantage. For that reason well contested examples are hard to find: the weaker side soon gives up the struggle in most cases. However, that does not affect the fundamental importance of pawn endings; for whenever the exchange of the last surviving pieces becomes a possibility it is essential to know what to do.

White displayed excellent judgment in allowing his opponent to exchange Rooks to reach the position shown in Diagram 123. As Black is the more aggressively placed,

123. The Extra Pawn Wins
The winning method is as follows: White first blocks the Q side; he then prevents the enemy King from breaking through in the centre; finally, he forces a passed pawn on the King's wing by advancing his KKtP.

the material advantage is almost offset. Play went on: 1 P-R4, K-Q5; 2 K-Q2, K-K4; 3 K-Q3, K-B4; 4 K-K2, K-K4; 5 K-B2, K-Q5; 6 P-KKt4, PxP e.p. ch; 7 KxP, K-K4; 8 K-Kt2 (but not 8 P-B4 ch, K-K5, when White is in *Zugzwang*), K-Q5; 9 P-B4, Resigns (after 9 . . . ,

K-K5; 10 K-Kt3, K-B4; 11 K-B3, K-B3; 12 K-K4 Black gets driven right back).

In pawn endings full use of the King is virtually automatic. That makes them a valuable training-ground for the endgame in general.

Minor-Piece Endings

Here too the stronger side can normally count on winning, though the defender naturally has more scope for resistance. In the case of Bishop versus Knight fluid or extended positions tend to favour the fast-moving Bishop, and of this the continuation from Diagram 124 is a good illustration.

124. A Decoy Pawn
White should not make a direct attempt to promote his QKtP. The right course is to use it to divert the opponent's pieces away from the centre and K side. That gives the white King a free hand there at the critical moment.

The game ended: **1 K-B3, K-K2; 2 K-K3, P-B3; 3 K-Q4, K-Q3; 4 B-Q1, Kt-Kt3; 5 B-B3, Kt-B1; 6 P-R4** (having improved the placing of his King and Bishop, White prepares to attack the enemy pawns), **Kt-K2; 7 B-K4, P-Kt4; 8 BPxP, BPxP; 9 PxP, PxP; 10 P-Kt6, P-Kt5** (if 10 . . . , Kt-B3 ch, then 11 BxKt gives a won pawn ending); **11 P-Kt7, K-B2; 12 K-K5, P-Kt6; 13 K-B4, Kt-Kt1; 14 KxP, Kt-B3; 15 B-B3, Kt-Q2; 16 K-B4, K-Q3; 17 K-B5, K-K2; 18 B-B6, Kt-Kt1; 19 B-Kt5, Resigns.**

Black was paralysed by the QKtP. The diversionary

power of such an 'outside' passed pawn is a highly significant factor in endgame play. It often proves decisive
when the material is level.

Major-Piece Endings

The great mobility and, therefore, defensive capacity of
the Queen and Rooks renders these endings the hardest
of all to win. A pawn carries little weight in comparison,
and positional advantages are much more likely to determine the result.

Although White is a pawn down in the position shown
in Diagram 125, the activity of his Rook enabled him to

125. White's Defences Held
By creating counter-threats
against the enemy KBP White
succeeded in reaching a theoretically drawn Rook ending
with four pawns versus three
on the same side. The extra
KP played practically no part
in the proceedings.

save the day. Play continued: **1 R-Kt7, P-Kt6; 2 K-Kt2,
RxP; 3 RxP, Q-B4; 4 R-Kt7, Q-Q4 ch; 5 Q-B3, QxQ ch;
6 KxQ, R-R6 ch; 7 K-K4, K-Kt2; 8 R-Kt5, K-B3; 9 R-B5,
R-R7; 10 K-K3, P-K4; 11 R-B7, K-K3; 12 R-Kt7, P-B3;
13 R-Kt8, K-B4; 14 R-KR8, R-R6 ch; 15 K-K2, K-K5; 16
R-QKt8, R-R7 ch; 17 K-B1, P-B4; 18 K-Kt2, K-Q6; 19
R-Kt3 ch, K-Q7; 20 R-K3, P-K5; 21 R-Kt3, K-K8; 22
R-Kt1 ch, K-K7; 23 R-Kt3, R-Q7; 24 R-R3, K-K8; 25
R-R1 ch, R-Q8; 26 R-R3,** and a draw was agreed.

White's consistently sound strategy was rewarded—the
endgame can be relied upon for a fair deal.

8

MODEL MASTER GAMES

While the theorists happily divide a game of chess into three parts, the practical player must learn to regard it as a unified whole, in which each phase flows smoothly and naturally into the next. The ability to maintain this rhythm in one's play—despite all the opponent's attempts to disturb it—is a mark of style, and it is this quality that most people find the hardest to acquire. Yet it need not be out of their reach. If they cannot pick it up from over-the-board contact with masters, they can do so by studying their games and the notes to them. A general 'feel' for good chess is soon developed.

The six games in this chapter have been chosen not only because they make excellent models but also in order to give the reader an insight into the history of top-level play and the progress in ideas and techniques in modern times. Each is a championship classic in its own right.

Lasker-Steinitz
Wilhelm Steinitz (1836-1900) became the first official World Champion when he beat Zukertort in 1886, though he had held the title unofficially for the previous twenty years. The conqueror of the romantic style, he worked out a system of strategic principles which is still recognised as the basis of modern chess.

Emanuel Lasker (1868-1941) defeated the ageing Steinitz in 1894 and went on to reign as World Champion for twenty-seven years. An indomitable fighter and great endgame player, he became a legend in his own lifetime.

9th Game, World Championship Match, Philadelphia, 1894. Ruy Lopez. *White*: Lasker. *Black*: Steinitz.

1 P-K4, P-K4; 2 Kt-KB3, Kt-QB3; 3 B-Kt5, P-Q3; 4 Kt-B3, P-QR3; 5 B-B4.

In the light of present-day opening knowledge White's last two moves seem very curious; they are hardly likely to preserve the initiative.

5 . . . , B-K3; 6 BxB, PxB; 7 P-Q4, PxP; 8 KtxP, KtxKt; 9 QxKt, Kt-K2; 10 B-Kt5, Kt-B3; 11 BxQ, KtxQ; 12 O-O-O, Kt-Kt4.

Simpler was 12 . . . , RxB; 13 RxKt, B-K2 with equality.

13 KtxKt, PxKt?*

Having little to worry him so far, Steinitz here gets too ambitious and strives for active play on the QR file; he only succeeds in weakening his pawns. 13 . . . , KxB left Black soundly placed.

14 BxP, RxP.

Rather better chances were offered by 14 . . . , R-R3; 15 P-K5, P-Q4; 16 P-QR3, K-Q2; 17 B-Q6, BxB; 18 PxB, KxP, since White's Bishop proves much superior to its opposite number.

15 B-Kt6, B-K2; 16 P-QB3, K-B2; 17 K-B2, KR-R1; 18 K-Kt3, QR-R5; 19 P-B3, KR-R3; 20 B-Q4, P-KKt3; 21 R-Q3, K-K1; 22 KR-Q1, P-K4?; 23 B-K3. (See Diagram 126.) 23 . . . , K-Q2; 24 B-B5, R-R8; 25 KR-Q2, K-K3; 26 B-R3, P-Kt4; 27 R-Q5, R-Kt3; 28 K-Kt4, P-Kt5.

Black bestirs himself, but this bid to obtain counterplay on the K side has come too late.

29 K-R5, R-R3 ch; 30 KxP, P-R4.

30 . . . , R-R8 would have caused more trouble. Now Black's one aggressive piece is exchanged off.

---

* A question mark is commonly used to denote a very bad move or mistake; an exclamation mark denotes a particularly strong or fine move.

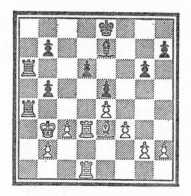

126. A Strategically Won Game

Black's 22nd move has weakened his position decisively. Now White will be able to occupy Q5 with a Rook and create unanswerable threats to the pawns at QKt4 and Q3. The black Rooks can achieve nothing on the QR file.

31 R-Q1, RxR; 32 RxR, PxP; 33 PxP, R-R1; 34 K-Kt6, R-KKt1; 35 KxP, R-Kt7; 36 P-R4, R-R7; 37 K-B6, BxP; 38 RxP ch, K-B2; 39 K-Q5, B-B3.

If 39 . . . , R-Q7 ch; 40 KxP, B-Kt6 ch; 41 P-B4, RxR; 42 BxR, P-R5, then 43 B-B5, P-R6; 44 B-Kt1, P-R7; 45 BxP and the pawns overwhelm the Bishop.

40 R-Q7 ch, K-Kt3; 41 K-K6.

The white King has dominated the endgame, first picking up the loose pawns on the Q side and now moving in for the kill on the other wing.

41 . . . , P-R5; 42 R-Q1, P-R6; 43 R-Kt1 ch, R-Kt7; 44 RxR ch, PxR; 45 B-B5, B-Q1; 46 P-Kt4, K-Kt4; 47 K-Q7, B-B3; 48 P-Kt5, K-B5; 49 P-Kt6, Resigns.

Alekhine-Capablanca

José Raoul Capablanca (1888-1942) was perhaps the most naturally gifted player the game has ever known. In his finest years he produced chess of sublime clarity and was virtually invincible, as witness his victory over Lasker in 1921 without the loss of a game.

Alexander Alekhine (1892-1946) caused universal surprise when he wrested the World Championship from Capablanca after a titanic, 34-game match in 1927. His great genius and competitive temperament enabled him to retain the title—except for the period 1935-1937—until his death.

34th Game, World Championship Match, Buenos Aires, 1927. Queen's Gambit Declined, Orthodox Defence. *White*: Alekhine. *Black*: Capablanca.

1 P-Q4, P-Q4; 2 P-QB4, P-K3; 3 Kt-QB3, Kt-KB3; 4 B-Kt5, QKt-Q2; 5 P-K3, P-B3; 6 P-QR3.

The main aim of this quiet move is to prevent any counterplay based on . . . . , B-Kt5.

6 . . . , B-K2; 7 Kt-B3, O-O; 8 B-Q3, PxP; 9 BxP, Kt-Q4; 10 BxB, QxB; 11 Kt-K4.

By avoiding the exchange of Knights White hopes to keep his opponent cramped. Alekhine had adopted the same idea in many of the earlier games of the match.

11 . . . , KKt-B3; 12 Kt-Kt3, P-B4; 13 O-O, Kt-Kt3; 14 B-R2, PxP; 15 KtxP, P-Kt3.

Black wants to be able to play . . . , P-K4 without surrendering his KB4 square to an enemy Knight.

16 R-B1, B-Q2; 17 Q-K2, QR-B1; 18 P-K4, P-K4; 19 Kt-B3, K-Kt2; 20 P-R3, P-KR3.

20 . . . , RxR; 21 RxR, R-B1 was the correct defensive method.

21 Q-Q2, B-K3?

Suddenly in difficulties, Capablanca falters and loses a pawn. He should have sought complications by 21 . . . , Kt-R5.

22 BxB, QxB; 23 Q-R5, Kt-B5; 24 QxRP, KtxKtP; 25 RxR, RxR; 26 QxP, Kt-B5; 27 Q-Kt4, R-QR1; 28 R-R1, Q-B3; 29 P-QR4!

It was essential to stop . . . , R-R5. The threat to the KP can be dealt with tactically.

29 . . . , KtxP; 30 KtxP.

White sees through the trap 30 KtxKt, QxKt; 31 R-QB1,

R-QB1; 32 KtxP?, when the double pin can be broken
by 32 . . . , Kt-K6!; 33 QxQ, RxR ch; 34 K-R2, Kt-B8 ch;
35 K-Kt1, Kt-Kt6 ch, recovering the Queen.

30 . . . , Q-Q3; 31 QxKt, QxKt; 32 R-K1, Kt-Q3; 33
Q-QB1, Q-B3; 34 Kt-K4, KtxKt; 35 RxKt.

**127. The Technical Phase
Begins**
The extra, outside passed
pawn constitutes a decisive
advantage, but the win requires skilful technique.
White's plan must be to
combine threats to advance
the QRP with attacks on the
enemy King, the position of
which has been weakened
slightly.

35 . . . , R-QKt1; 36 R-K2, R-QR1; 37 R-R2, R-R4;
38 Q-B7, Q-R3; 39 Q-B3 ch, K-R2; 40 R-Q2, Q-Kt3.
White was threatening R-Q8.

41 R-Q7, Q-Kt8 ch; 42 K-R2, Q-Kt1 ch; 43 P-Kt3,
R-KB4; 44 Q-Q4, Q-K1; 45 R-Q5, R-B6.
In a Queen ending Black would have no answer to the
QRP.

46 P-R4, Q-KR1; 47 Q-Kt6.
The exchange of Queens is incorrect if, as is the case at
the moment, Black can post his Rook in the ideal position
behind the passed pawn, thereby holding it up permanently.

47 . . . , Q-R8; 48 K-Kt2, R-B3; 49 Q-Q4!
Having forced the Rook to retire to guard the King,
White happily gets rid of the Queens.

49 . . . , QxQ; 50 RxQ, K-Kt2.
If 50 . . . , R-R3, the white King marches straight
across to the Q side to support the pawn.

51 P-QR5, R-R3; **52** R-Q5, R-KB3; **53** R-Q4, R-R3; **54** R-R4.

Now White's Rook is ideally placed and Black's is reduced to passivity.

54 . . . , K-B3; **55** K-B3, K-K4; **56** K-K3, P-R4; **57** K-Q3, K-Q4; **58** K-B3, K-B4; **59** R-R2, K-Kt4; **60** R-Kt2 ch, K-B4.

The QRP would have fulfilled its decoying role after **60** . . . , KxP; **61** R-R2 ch, K-Kt4; **62** RxR, KxR; **63** K-Q4 with a won pawn ending.

61 R-R2, K-Kt4; **62** K-Q4, R-Q3 ch; **63** K-K5, R-K3 ch; **64** K-B4, K-R3.

Black has managed to free his Rook, but his K-side pawns are at the mercy of the white King.

65 K-Kt5, R-K4 ch; **66** K-R6, R-KB4; **67** P-B4, R-B4; **68** R-R3, R-B2; **69** K-Kt7, R-Q2; **70** P-B5.

Strong though this thrust is, it would have been even stronger preceded by K-B6.

70 . . . , PxP; **71** K-R6, P-B5; **72** PxP, R-Q4; **73** K-Kt7, R-KB4; **74** R-R4, K-Kt4; **75** R-K4!, K-R3; **76** K-R6.

Black's desperate struggle nears its end. He is in *Zugzwang* and cannot avoid the loss of his remaining pawns; for example, **76** . . . , K-Kt2; **77** R-K5, RxP; **78** K-Kt5, R-B8; **79** KxP, P-B4; **80** K-Kt5, P-B5; **81** R-KB5, P-B6; **82** K-Kt4 etc.

76 . . . , RxRP; **77** R-K5, R-R8; **78** KxP, R-KKt8; **79** R-KKt5, R-KR8; **80** R-KB5, K-Kt3; **81** RxP, K-B3; **82** R-K7, Resigns.

Euwe-Smyslov

Dr. Max Euwe (b. 1901) championed academic correctness of style. This and deep theoretical knowledge brought him his success against Alekhine in 1935, but two years later the former Champion, showing more respect for the opposition, regained the title convincingly.

Vasily Smyslov (b. 1921) combines artistry and superb technique. Second in the World Championship Tournament in 1948, he finally gained the crown in 1957 only to lose it the following year. In recent events Smyslov has again displayed challenging form.

Round 24, World Championship Tournament, Moscow, 1948. Queen's Pawn, Grünfeld Defence. *White*: Euwe. *Black*: Smyslov.

1 P-Q4, Kt-KB3; 2 P-QB4, P-KKt3; 3 Kt-QB3, P-Q4; 4 Kt-B3, B-Kt2; 5 Q-Kt3, PxP; 6 QxBP, O-O; 7 P-K4, B-Kt5; 8 B-K3, KKt-Q2; 9 Q-Kt3, Kt-Kt3; 10 P-QR4.

Dr Euwe repeats the line with which he had been successful against the same opponent in an earlier round. Better prepared this time, Smyslov shows that the weakening of White's QKt4 can be exploited.

10 . . . , P-QR4; 11 P-Q5.

Sounder is 11 R-Q1, leaving the centre pawns uncommitted.

11 . . . , BxKKt; 12 PxB, Q-Q3!; 13 Kt-Kt5.

After 13 BxKt, PxB; 14 Kt-Kt5, Q-K4 White is very weak on the black squares.

13 . . . , Q-Kt5 ch; 14 QxQ, PxQ; 15 KtxP.

15 P-R5 is inadequate on account of 15 . . . , BxP; 16 R-R2 (or 16 R-QKt1, Kt-R5), B-K4; 17 P-B4, B-Q3; 18 P-K5, P-Kt6! . . . .

15 . . . , RxP; 16 R-QKt1, KKt-Q2; 17 Kt-Kt5, R-B1; 18 B-K2.

The safest plan was to recentralise the Knight by 18 Kt-Q4, whereupon there is nothing better than 18 . . . , P-Kt6; 19 KtxP, R-Kt5; 20 Kt-Q2, RxKtP with approximately equal chances.

18 . . . , P-Kt6; 19 Kt-R3.

White decides to give up a pawn to ease the growing pressure on the Q side. However, such a step was not really necessary, and preferable seems 19 B-Q2, intending to answer 19 . . . , R-B7 by 20 B-Q1, RxP; 21 RxR, BxR; 22 BxP with a tenable game.

19 . . . , BxP; 20 RxB, RxKt; 21 K-Q2.

128. Bishops versus Knights
In aiming for this position White hoped that the potential strength of his two Bishops would offset the lost pawn. But, unfortunately, the inflexibility of his pawn formation restricts the Bishops yet leaves the Knights unfettered.

21 . . . , Kt-R3; 22 KR-QKt1, QKt-B4; 23 B-Q4.

If he attacks the advanced QKtP a third time by 23 B-Q1, then 23 . . . , R-R7 is strong.

23 . . . , P-K4; 24 PxP e.p., KtxP; 25 B-K3, Kt(Q2)-B4; 26 BxKt.

To surrender one of the Bishops is a sign of despair, but the Knights were becoming more threatening with every move.

26 . . . , KtxB; 27 K-B3, R-R5; 28 K-Q2, K-Kt2, K-Kt2; 29 K-K3, R-Q1; 30 R-QB1, P-Kt3; 31 B-B4, KR-QR1; 32 B-Q5.

32 BxKtP failed against 32 . . . , R-Kt5, a tactical point made possible by Black's foresight in placing his King out of the Bishop's reach.

32 . . . , R-R7; 33 R(B1)-QKt1, KR-R5; 34 K-Q2, R-Q5 ch; 35 K-K2, Kt-R5!

The game ends with a fine combination.

36 RxR, PxR; 37 R-QR1.

If 37 BxRP, then 37 . . . , Kt-B6 ch; 38 K-K3, R-R5; 39 B-Kt3, R-R6, winning a piece.
   37 . . . , Kt-B6 ch; 38 K-K3, R-Q8; Resigns.

Botvinnik-Tal

Mikhail Botvinnik (b. 1911) won the vacant world title in 1948 and held it—but for two twelve-month periods—until 1963. He owed his supremacy to unsurpassed powers as a strategist, great endgame skill and a dedicated, scientific approach.

Mikhail Tal (b. 1936) became the youngest ever World Champion when he beat Botvinnik in 1960. He rose to fame on a crest of combinations and sensational games, but since his defeat in the return match his genius, sapped by ill-health, has waned. Nevertheless, Tal remains a leading championship contender.

9th Game, World Championship Match, Moscow, 1961. English. *White*: Botvinnik. *Black*: Tal.
   1 P-QB4, Kt-KB3; 2 Kt-QB3, P-K4; 3 P-KKt3, P-B3; 4 Kt-B3, P-K5; 5 Kt-Q4, P-Q4; 6 PxP, Q-Kt3.
It is typical of Tal to choose an aggressive line even as Black—he is never afraid of taking a risk.
   7 Kt-Kt3, PxP; 8 B-Kt2, P-QR4.
This attempt to attack is going too far. He ought to have consolidated in the centre, where he is already heavily committed.
   9 P-Q3, P-R5; 10 B-K3, Q-Kt5; 11 Kt-Q4, P-R6; 12 Kt-B2, QxP; 13 B-Q4, B-QKt5; 14 KtxB, QxKt; 15 BxKt, PxB; 16 O-O.
Botvinnik has lured his opponent to his downfall. Black has won a useless pawn at a huge cost in time and position.
   16 . . . , B-K3; 17 R-B1, Kt-B3; 18 PxP, PxP; 19 KtxP, BxP; 20 Kt-Q6 ch, K-B1; 21 KtxKtP, Kt-K4; 22 Kt-B5, R-QKt1.

135

129. Moment of Decision
As the black King is so badly placed, a natural plan for White is to launch a direct attack combining Q-Q6 ch and advancing the KBP and KP. But Botvinnik, unwilling to give Tal a chance to complicate, decides to play for the endgame.

23 Kt-R6, B-Kt6; 24 KtxQ, BxQ; 25 KRxB, RxKt; 26 R-R1, R-Kt7.

If Black tries to defend his QRP by 26 . . . , R-QR5, then 27 P-B4 followed by R-Q7, threatening B-Q5, is too strong.

27 K-B1, K-Kt2; 28 RxP.

This ending is clearly won for White; for although all the pawns are on one side, which is to the defender's advantage, Black's are broken and weak. It is merely a matter of time.

28 . . . , R-QB1; 29 B-K4, R-K1; 30 R-R4, R-K2; 31 B-B5, R-B2; 32 R-R4, P-R3; 33 R-R4, R-B4; 34 P-R3, Kt-B5; 35 B-Q3, Kt-K4; 36 B-K4, Kt-B5; 37 B-Q3, Kt-K4; 38 B-K4, Kt-B5; 39 K-K1, Kt-K4; 40 R(R4)-Q4, R-B6; 41 R(Q1)-Q2, R-B8 ch; 42 R-Q1, R-B6; 43 P-B4.

At last, having carried out much painstaking regrouping, White begins to push forward. Tal reacts by throwing in a second pawn, but it is only bluff.

43 . . . , P-B4; 44 BxP, Kt-B5; 45 R(Q4)-Q3, R(B6)-B7; 46 B-Kt4, R-R7; 47 R-Kt3, K-Kt3; 48 K-B2, Kt-Q7; 49 R-K3, Kt-B5; 50 R-Kt3, Kt-Q7; 51 R-K3, Kt-B5; 52 R-K8, Kt-Q7; 53 R-K5, K-B3; 54 R-B5 ch, K-Kt3; 55 R-K5, K-B3; 56 B-R5, R-B6; 57 P-R4, R-B5; 58 B-B3, R(B5)-B7;

59 B-Q5, R-R5; 60 B-B3, R(R5)-R7; 61 R-K1, R-R5; 62 P-R5, R-B6; 63 B-Kt2, R-B7; 64 R-Q1, R-R6; 65 B-Q5, R-R5; 66 K-K1.

Now Black is unable to avoid the exchange of a pair of Rooks, after which his powers of resistance collapse.

66 . . . , R-Q5; 67 B-Kt2, Kt-Kt6; 68 RxR, KtxR; 69 K-B2, Kt-K3; 70 B-K4, R-Kt7; 71 R-B5 ch, K-Kt2; 72 R-Q5, K-B3; 73 K-B3, Resigns.

Spassky-Petrosian

Tigran Petrosian (b. 1929) succeeded Botvinnik in 1963 and reigned for six years. Renowned for his defensive virtuosity and subtle manoeuvring in balanced positions, he has given a new breadth to strategic thinking.

Boris Spassky (b. 1937) has the same flexible, realistic attitude as Petrosian but in style is more incisive. He won the world title at his second challenge, in 1969, and three years later had in turn to give way to a younger man. He could well make a comeback.

7th Game, World Championship Match, Moscow, 1966. Torre Attack. *White*: Spassky. *Black:* Petrosian.

1 P-Q4, Kt-KB3; 2 Kt-KB3, P-K3; 3 B-Kt5, P-Q4; 4 QKt-Q2, B-K2; 5 P-K3, QKt-Q2; 6 B-Q3, P-B4; 7 P-B3.

One of White's objects in this quiet opening is to solidify the position in the centre in order eventually to build up a K-side attack. Well aware of this, Black delays castling.

7 . . . , P-QKt3; 8 O-O, B-Kt2; 9 Kt-K5, KtxKt; 10 PxKt, Kt-Q2; 11 B-KB4.

Safer was 11 BxB, QxB; 12 P-KB4, P-B3; 13 Q-R5 ch with a likely draw. The text move provokes tense, double-edged play.

11 . . . , Q-B2; 12 Kt-B3, P-KR3; 13 P-QKt4, P-KKt4;

14 B-Kt3, P-KR4; 15 P-KR4, KtPxP; 16 B-KB4, O-O-O; 17 P-R4.

Spassky has not made the most of his chances: for one thing, sacrificing the KRP was unnecessary; for another, the advance of the QRP should have been preceded by PxP. Now Black can block the Queen's wing completely.

17 . . . , P-B5; 18 B-K2, P-R3; 19 K-R1, QR-Kt1; 20 R-KKt1, R-Kt5; 21 Q-Q2, KR-Kt1; 22 P-R5, P-Kt4; 23 QR-Q1, B-B1; 24 Kt-R2, KtxP!; 25 KtxR, PxKt.

In two pawns and dangerous threats against the enemy King Black has more than enough compensation for the exchange.

26 P-K4, B-Q3; 27 Q-K3, Kt-Q2; 28 BxB, QxB; 29 R-Q4, P-K4; 30 R-Q2, P-B4!

130. Pawn Avalanche
Black's all-embracing strategy approaches its climax. Having eliminated any risk of being attacked himself, he is free to throw everything into the offensive. The line of pawns will sweep down upon the enemy King and smother it.

31 PxQP, P-B5; 32 Q-K4, Kt-B3; 33 Q-B5 ch, K-Kt1; 34 P-B3, B-B1; 35 Q-Kt1, P-Kt6; 36 R-K1, P-R6; 37 B-B1, R-R1; 38 PxP, BxP; 39 K-Kt1, BxB; 40 KxB, P-K5; 41 Q-Q1, Kt-Kt5!

A Knight sacrifice adds a final, elegant touch.

42 PxKt, P-B6; 43 R-KKt2, PxR ch; Resigns.

Fischer-Spassky

Robert Fischer (b. 1943) is considered by most experts to be the greatest chessplayer we have yet seen. He became the eleventh World Chess Champion after his dramatic victory over Spassky in the 'Match of the Century' in 1972 and has claimed that he will retain his supremacy for over thirty years.

In Fischer's play modern chess has reached new peaks of excellence. His strengths include a deep knowledge of opening theory, mastery of middlegame strategy, clear and rapid tactical insight, superb endgame technique and a fierce determination to win and reap his just rewards. It is hard to imagine how anyone can beat him.

10th Game, World Championship Match, Reykjavik, 1972. Ruy Lopez. *White:* Fischer. *Black:* Spassky.

1 P-K4, P-K4; 2 Kt-KB3, Kt-QB3; 3 B-Kt5, P-QR3; 4 B-R4, Kt-B3; 5 O-O, B-K2; 6 R-K1, P-QKt4; 7 B-Kt3, P-Q3; 8 P-B3, O-O; 9 P-KR3, Kt-Kt1; 10 P-Q4, QKt-Q2; 11 QKt-Q2, B-Kt2; 12 B-B2, R-K1.

All this is typical of the latest methods of handling the Ruy Lopez. White now goes for expansion on the Q side.

13 P-QKt4, B-KB1; 14 P-QR4, Kt-Kt3; 15 P-R5, QKt-Q2; 16 B-Kt2, Q-Kt1; 17 R-Kt1, P-B4.

Spassky rightly chooses active defence and does not shrink from an open tactical battle.

18 KtPxP, QPxP; 19 PxKP, QKtxP; 20 KtxKt, QxKt; 21 P-QB4, Q-B5; 22 BxKt, QxB; 23 PxP.

Fischer has acquired a pawn, but it has cost him his fine fianchettoed Bishop. Black's simplest course, both here and on the next move, was . . . , PxP followed by . . . , B-R3, obtaining lively counterplay.

23 . . . , KR-Q1; 24 Q-B1, Q-QB6; 25 Kt-B3, QxP; 26 B-Kt3!, PxP; 27 Q-KB4, R-Q2; 28 Kt-K5, Q-B2; 29 QR-Q1!

131. Attacking Climax
While Black was picking up pawns on the Q side Fischer was switching his forces to the other wing for an attack on his opponent's KB2 point. The directness and power of the threats remind one irresistibly of Morphy's combinations. The defence is very difficult.

29 ..., R-K2; 30 BxP ch, RxB; 31 QxR ch, QxQ; 32 KtxQ, BxP; 33 RxB, KxKt; 34 R-Q7 ch, K-B3; 35 R-Kt7, R-R8 ch.

Checking does not help Black. It was better to play 35 ..., P-Kt5 and keep the Rook at the back to defend and support the passed pawns.

36 K-R2, B-Q3 ch; 37 P-Kt3, P-Kt5; 38 K-Kt2, P-R4; 39 R-Kt6, R-Q8; 40 K-B3, K-B2.

Black has almost a material equality, but in positional terms he is at a big disadvantage; for his Q-side pawns are immobilised and the Bishop can do nothing to counter White's activity on the white squares.

41 K-K2, R-Q4; 42 P-B4, P-Kt3; 43 P-Kt4, PxP; 44 PxP, P-Kt4; 45 P-B5, B-K4; 46 R-Kt5!, K-B3.

If 46 ..., B-Q5, then 47 R-K6 is decisive.

47 KRxP, B-Q5; 48 R-Kt6 ch, K-K4; 49 K-B3!

Fischer concludes the game prettily. Black is helpless against the threats from the white Rooks.

49 ..., R-Q1; 50 R-Kt8, R-Q2; 51 R(Kt4)-Kt7, R-Q3; 52 R-Kt6, R-Q2; 53 R-Kt6, K-Q4; 54 RxP, B-K4; 55 P-B6, K-Q5; 56 R-Kt1, Resigns.

9

OTHER ASPECTS OF CHESS

It is a commonly held belief that chess has nothing more
to offer than hours · of concentration against a silent
opponent. Perhaps there was some truth in this a century
or longer ago, but a few minutes spent at a modern
tournament should be enough to convince anyone that
there is none now. Competitive chess has, in its own way,
at least as much excitement and drama as any sport, and
the increasing number of people not only who play it but
who go to watch is evidence.

Organisation
The step from occasional games at home with a friend to
more serious play is very easy to take; for chess is highly
organised at all levels, from local to international. In
Britain most towns worthy of the name have a chess club,
and these compete against each other in leagues based
either on major cities or individual counties. The counties
in turn join to form regional groups, while an overall
control is administered by the British Chess Federation
(in Scotland by the Scottish Chess Association and in
Wales by the Welsh Chess Union).

The B.C.F. is directly responsible for running the
national championships and for choosing players and
teams to represent the country in international events. It
also forms, through its affiliation, a constituent part of
the *Fédération Internationale des Échecs* (International
Chess Federation), the game's governing body.

Thanks to the F.I.D.É. world chess is efficiently and

amicably controlled. Once upon a time the World Champion looked on the title as virtually his personal property and often avoided challengers—particularly, dangerous ones—if his conditions were not fulfilled. Now he is obliged to play a match every third year against the winner of a carefully graduated series of qualifying events. The programme is tough but fair. In many ordinary ways the work of the F.I.D.É. touches every chessplayer: in the very laws and codes, for instance, by which a game is conducted. Universally recognised, these are constantly being revised and perfected to the general good.

Writing

Being so suitable for preservation on paper, chess has built up over hundreds of years a cultural heritage that many of the sciences would be proud of. Classic works like Philidor's *L'Analyze des Échecs* (*The Analysis of Chess*), published in 1749, Staunton's *The Chess-Player's Handbook* (1847) and Nimzovitch's *Mein System* (*My System*), published in 1925, made a great impact on the development of the game and may still be read with profit. The authors' ideas, if not all their analysis, remain valid.

Today more is being written than ever. Most countries boast a periodical (the United Kingdom has two of international repute: *The British Chess Magazine* and *Chess*), while rarely a month passes without an important book being brought out somewhere. Writing has become the medium through which the expert can best make a contribution to chess; for in the playing arena destructive realism is often better rewarded than creativity.

To conclude, here is a selection of books for further reading. It is confined to those in English, though language barriers are easily overcome—at least, where games are concerned—thanks to the widely used 'algebraic' notation (in this every square has a simple reference, from 'a1' to 'h8', calculated from White's side and from left to right, thus White's QR1 is a1 and his K4 is e4, while Black's K4 is e5).

Lasker, Em. *Lasker's Manual of Chess*; Fine, R. *The Ideas behind the Chess Openings*; Evans, L. and Korn, W. *Modern Chess Openings* (Tenth Edition); Euwe, Dr M. and Kramer, H. *The Middle Game* (2 vols.); Euwe, Dr M. and Hooper, David. *A Guide to Chess Endings*; Golombek, H. *Capablanca's* 100 *Best Games of Chess*; Alekhine, Dr A. *My Best Games of Chess*, 1908-1923 and *My Best Games of Chess*, 1924-1937; Clarke, P. H. *Petrosian's Best Games of Chess*, 1946-1963. Fischer, Bobby *My* 60 *Memorable Games*; Botvinnik, M. M. *Championship Chess*; Golombek, H. *The World Chess Championship* 1948; Alexander, C. H. O'D. *Fischer v. Spassky: Reykjavik* 1972; Bouwmeester, H. *Modern End-Game Studies for the Chess-Player*; Lipton, Michael, Matthews, R. C. O. and Rice, John *Chess Problems: Introduction to an Art*; Murray, H. J. R. *A Short History of Chess*.

Index